Borders, Bodies and Narratives of Crisis in Europe

Thanasis Lagios • Vasia Lekka
Grigoris Panoutsopoulos

Borders, Bodies and Narratives of Crisis in Europe

palgrave
macmillan

Thanasis Lagios
National and Kapodistrian University of Athens
Athens, Greece

Vasia Lekka
Hellenic Open University
Patras, Greece

Grigoris Panoutsopoulos
National and Kapodistrian University of Athens
Athens, Greece

ISBN 978-3-319-75585-4 ISBN 978-3-319-75586-1 (eBook)
https://doi.org/10.1007/978-3-319-75586-1

Library of Congress Control Number: 2018936612

Cover credit: Modern building window © saulgranda/Getty

Printed on acid-free paper

This Palgrave Pivot imprint is published by the registered company Springer International Publishing AG part of Springer Nature.
The registered company address is: Gewerbestrasse 11, 6330 Cham, Switzerland

To all those who were condemned to death in front of the Western borders; to all those who were excluded from life due to their lack of credibility in front of another capitalist crisis; for, as Walter Benjamin has warned us, "even the dead will not be safe from the enemy if he wins. And this enemy has not ceased to be victorious"

Preface

During the past few years, as subjects that live, work and speak in Greece, namely, at the borders of what is called "Europe" and at the heart of what is called "debt crisis", we have witnessed, on the one hand, bodies that struggle to survive crossing the borders, in order to have the opportunity to live, work and speak in what is called "First World", and, on the other hand, the intensification and reproduction of specific narratives on a Europe under "crisis". It is a crisis that has been described as economic, ideological, political, humanist or humanitarian, to name but a few, since its worldwide repercussions and consequences have been manifold. To be sure, this is not the first time that the eruption of a crisis has led both subjects and bodies to a practical and theoretical impasse. However, in Western societies of late capitalism, after the 1989–1991 collapse of State Socialism and the emergence of narratives about the so-called End of History, as well as after the downfall of the neoliberal free-market utopia in 2008, it might be the first time that what Adorno had said to Horkheimer in a discussion, entitled "Diskussion über Theorie und Praxis" ("Discussion over Theory and Praxis", 1956), has gained its full significance and could be seen as absolutely timely: "We do not live in a revolutionary situation, and actually things are worse than ever. What is horrifying is that for the first time we live in a world in which it is not possible to imagine things getting better".

Within this frame, it becomes all the more necessary and crucial not only to raise questions regarding the crisis *per se* and its distinct characteristics and ramifications at different levels, but, primarily, to delineate its genealogy. For, from our point of view, the fact that another "crisis" has erupted in capitalist societies does not constitute a surprise; a crisis that, once again, condemns to death specific forms of life and produces specific forms of subjectivity; a crisis that sometimes annuls and, other times, allows specific forms of resistance. The only "surprising" thing in this case is that there has dominated a denial to realise and confess the theoretical impasse, as well as an unwillingness to raise questions regarding the recent crisis, its preconditions and its consequences.

This book consists of two Parts, born on the margins of this crisis and its experiences. From this perspective, it focuses on three interrelated signifiers and their historicity: *capitalism—crisis—subject*. It is these three signifiers that constitute the thread linking the two Parts, despite the different starting points and possibly different paths; nonetheless, we hope that their "difference" is not "a difference of object or domain, but of point of attack, perspective, and delimitation", as Foucault remarked in his inaugural lecture in December 1970 at the Collège de France. The starting point in Part I, entitled *Within the Walls: Transformations of Migration Control and Management*, is the recent political, economic, discursive and technoscientific transformations in migration control and management. Migrants' exploitation as a useful labour force in capitalist societies, migration's representation as a "humanist crisis" and the concomitant militarisation of its control and management, borders' technoscientific transformations and diffusion in the body politic, migrants' categorisation as bodies that eventually "do not matter" and as lives "unworthy of life" within twenty-first-century biopolitical societies are some of the key issues discussed in Part I. The starting point in Part II, entitled *Humanist or Capitalist Crisis? Notes and Remarks Concerning a False Dilemma*, is the 2007–8 financial and political crisis. The discussion revolves around a critique of the dilemma between "capitalist" or "humanist" crisis, since a genealogy of the discourses on crisis and of critical discourse shows a paradoxical displacement of signifiers: while the crisis was initially interpreted as a "capitalist" one, very soon a displacement of the signifiers took place, and its interpretation as "humanist" became the dominant one, leading to the obfuscation and oblivion of the very conditions of possibility of the link between *capitalism—crisis—subject* in Modernity. Hence, both Parts deal critically with the three signifiers *capitalism—crisis—subject*, under the genealogical prism of a "history of the present", since an attempt to understand modernity is an attempt to sketch a historical ontology of ourselves and, conversely, to sketch a historical ontology of ourselves is to raise once again the historical-philosophical question *par excellence*, as Foucault attempted regarding the Kantian question: *What is Enlightenment*?

In sum, this book does not aim at giving answers and offering solutions, but at raising *questions*, within the historical context of a condition that seems, *prima facie*, highly desperate. For, it might be extremely desperate to try to *answer* questions that seem—and, in fact, are—obsolete, while it might be more fruitful—both theoretically and politically—to raise questions, even though the answers have not been yet articulated. And, it is exactly for this reason that why it is, to our view, extremely pivotal to contribute to the widening of the discussion and the enriching of the questions regarding the current crisis within capitalist societies. For, as V.I. Lenin wrote, more than a century ago, on the eve of another historical crisis, when the established order was put into question, in an article entitled "L.N. Tolstoy and the Modern Labour Movement" (1910): "Despair is typical of those who do not understand the causes of evil, see no way out, and are incapable of struggle".

* * *

This book is an elaborated version of the book *Borders' Diffusion, Bodies' Inscription, Points of Inscription* [*Διάχυση Συνόρων, Χάραξη Σωμάτων, Σημεία Καταγραφής*], published by futura Publishing House, in June 2016, in Athens (Greece). Even though it is a collective work, born on the margins of the authors' common thoughts, discussions and experiences, it should be mentioned that Chaps. 1, 2 and 4 (Part I) are written by Vasia Lekka and Grigoris Panoutsopoulos, Chaps. 3, 5 and 6 (Part I) are written by Vasia Lekka, and Chaps. 7, 8, 9 and 10 (Part II) are written by Thanasis Lagios.

Athens, Greece

Thanasis Lagios
Vasia Lekka
Grigoris Panoutsopoulos

Contents

PART I

Within the Walls: Transformations of Migration Control and Management

CHAPTER 1

Introduction: Within the Walls[1]

Abstract This chapter is a short introduction into the subject of Part I of the present book, having as a point of departure the recent transformations in European border and migration politics. Through a series of critical questions, the key points regarding the so-called migration crisis will be presented.

Keywords Migration • Walls • Border politics • Documenta 14 Athens/Kassel

"You have come to Greece to make art visible and graciously offered to purchase the participation of invisible exoticized others. We're flattered. Your stone is supposed to give us a voice, to speak to our stories. But rocks can't talk! We can! We have stolen your stone and we will not give it back. Your stone may be languishing without papers in a prison on the island of Samos. Your stone may have drowned and sunk to the bottom of the Mediterranean [...]. Your stone may have been deported to Turkey [...]. Your stone may be on a flight to Sweden with its new 2,000 euro fake passport. Your stone may be driven to suicide in Moria detention center desperate for freedom. Your stone may be waiting in line

[1] The title was inspired by the 2008 French film *Entre les murs* (*Within the walls*), based on the 2006 novel written by François Bégaudeau.

T. Lagios et al., *Borders, Bodies and Narratives of Crisis in Europe*,
https://doi.org/10.1007/978-3-319-75586-1_1

outside the offices of Katehaki,[2] [...]. Your stone may be selling its body to strangers in Pedion Tou Areos.[3] Your stone may be legally recognized as a refugee but sleeping on the street. You have asked us to perform a fake funeral for your stones. We've had more than our fair share of funerals. [...]. Governments and NGOs have been pulling our strings, making decisions for us for far too long. But we are cutting the strings, dancing on our own, speaking louder than any stone" (LGBTQI Refugees GR 2017).

With these words, "LGBTQI Refugees GR" decided to protest against the artistic performance by the Spanish artist Roger Bernat, for the international art exhibition *Documenta 14 Athens/Kassel*. Bernat constructed a replica of the "oath stone", in front of which the trial of Socrates was held in 399 BC (Bernat 2017). This stone would perform a symbolic function: socially excluded groups would carry the stone into the city of Athens in a factitious funeral, before the stone's scheduled journey to Kassel to be buried at Thingplatz. Through this "ritual", founded, *inter alia*, on an Orientalist version of the "freedom of speech", these "invisible" groups would supposedly acquire a temporary visibility. It is exactly for these reasons that this group of migrants decided to "steal" the artwork and release the above statement. Their words are exceptionally penetrative, revealing the superficiality and often hypocrisy of the Western humanist discourse that is usually reproducing the dominant stereotypes about migrants and, consequently, their exploitation.

Since 2015, as an aftermath of the war in Syria, migration has been, more than ever before, at the heart of the EU dominant discourse and politics. As the *Documenta* event indicates, stones and other artistic creations about migrants may be free to cross the European borders, but migrants themselves are not; on the contrary, they are condemned to remain silent and invisible. And even though we did witness a short period of "open" borders when refugees were supposedly welcomed in the Western world, a series of highly significant transformations has taken place in European migration politics, during the last few years. The following key events are, among others, quite indicative. In September 2015, Hungary decided to build a fence along its borders with Serbia, rendering illegal border crossing punishable with imprisonment and expulsion; a few days later, a site of Dachau concentration

[2] Katehaki is the street where the Attica Regional Asylum Office is located.

[3] Pedion Tou Areos is one of the largest public parks in the centre of Athens.

camp in Germany—the first Nazi concentration camp opened on 22 March 1933,[4] whose gate was decorated with the notorious slogan "Arbeit macht frei"—was transformed into detention centre for refugees; already, during the period 2012–2014, Greece had built a fence along its borders in Evros, whereas a series of camps and detention centres for migrants was built all over the country. Since most migrants were represented as "illegal", all these practices were reinforced both politically and financially by the EU, whereas only a few "humanist" voices in favour of migrants' *human* rights were heard all over Europe. Therefore, during the last few years, many fences have been built along the borders of several European countries, the European borders have been closed and the path towards the "European dream" has been blocked, while thousands of migrants have been restrained in the European periphery, in "neutral zones", as well as in Middle Eastern countries. From this perspective, a series of significant questions arises.

In fact, which similarities does the twenty-first-century European map have to a painting by Amedeo Modigliani?[5] To what extent have borders' disposition and function been transformed during the last years, when even the signifier "Schengenized" (Snyder 2005) has lost its meaning, since exclusion does not refer exclusively to Europe's

[4] Despite the fact that it was the Nazis who first introduced concentration camps as a "scientific" method of industrial extermination (mostly, through the creation of the notorious "extermination camps" during World War II), it should be noted that concentration camps have been part of Western civilisation long before Hitler. Probably, the first concentration camp was built by the Spaniards in Cuba, in 1896. Imprisonment in concentration camps was also used by the English against the Boers, during the early twentieth century, as well as by the Germans in their attempt to colonise Southwest Africa, exterminating over 100,000 people during the period 1904–1907. In Germany, the first concentration camp (*Konzentrationslager*) appeared during the Social-Democratic governance. More specifically, after the 1923 Declaration of the state of exception, thousands of communists were imprisoned in concentration camps, on the basis of the Schutzhaft, whose origin lies in the Prussian law of 4 June 1851. In the same context, a refugee camp (*Konzentrationslager für Ausländer*) was then created at Cottbus-Sielow, for the imprisonment of Jewish refugees from Eastern countries. According to Agamben, it may be considered as the first concentration camp for Jews in the twentieth century—even though, under no circumstances could it be considered as an extermination camp (Agamben 1998).

[5] In his attempt to describe the nineteenth-century political map, Ernest Gellner writes: "Look now instead at the ethnographic and political map of an area of the modem world. It resembles not Kokoschka, but, say, Modigliani. There is very little shading; neat flat surfaces are clearly separated from each other, it is generally plain where one begins and another ends, and there is little if any ambiguity or overlap" (1983: 139–140).

external borders? What could actually imply borders' intensified militarisation, digitisation and diffusion, through a series of novel technoscientific means and practices? Within which historical *a priori* has the human body been transformed into the *par excellence* carrier of the border, into *the* "password",[6] that is going to ensure to someone his/her entrance and integration within contemporary societies of control? After all, by whom—and, more importantly, for whom—has the Western world been built? For, even though it is usually represented as a "borderless world", it is actually founded on dichotomies, such as between "natives" and "foreigners", "legal" and "illegal", "refugees" and "migrants". And, what is the price that migrants have to pay for their entrance into this "borderless world" that offers its hospitality exclusively to those bodies that, "in materializing the norm, qualify as bodies that matter" (Butler 1993: 16)? Within which historical procedures have migrants' dead bodies in the Mediterranean Sea become a constitutive condition of our reality? Within the frame of biopolitical power, of this "power's hold over life" (Foucault 2003: 239) that has marked Western societies since the end of the eighteenth century, how could we endure to witness—once again, in history—these "corpses without death", these "non-humans whose decease is debased into a matter of serial production" (Agamben 1999: 72)? All in all, which could be the forms of our critique towards the "humanist discourse" that is repeatedly articulated after tragedies, such as the one in Lampedusa in 2013, at the exact same time that new, harsher measures to deal with the "humanist crisis" are designed, decided and approved, whereas almost all declarations of human rights do, in reality, address exclusively to the most privileged part of humanity, exempting those not deemed to belong to it? In sum, our purpose is to raise these questions, to understand their significance, and to try to re-read and re-interpret migration control and management during the last few years, so as to highlight the fact that migrants, even though they "should have incarnated the rights of man par excellence", constitute, on the contrary, "the radical crisis of this concept" (Agamben 1995: 116).

[6] Following Gilles Deleuze, Dijstelbloem et al. have argued that "[i]n a society that focuses on control, the body gradually becomes a 'password'" (2011: 13). See also, Deleuze (1992).

References

Agamben, G. 1995. "We Refugees". *Symposium: A Quarterly Journal in Modern Literature*, 49(2): 114–119.

Agamben, G. 1998. *Homo Sacer. Sovereign Power and Bare Life*, tr. D. Heller-Roazen. Stanford, CA: Stanford University Press.

Agamben, G. 1999. *Remnants of Auschwitz. The Witness and the Archive*, tr. D. Heller-Roazen. New York: Zone Books.

Bernat, R. 2017. "The Place of the Thing". http://rogerbernat.info/en/shows/the-place-of-the-thing/ (Accessed 26 November 2017).

Butler, J. 1993. *Bodies That Matter. On the Discursive Limits of "Sex"*. New York/London: Routledge.

Deleuze, G. 1992. "Postscript on the Societies of Control". *October*, 59: 3–7.

Dijstelbloem, H., Meijer, A., and Besters, M. 2011. "The Migration Machine". In H. Dijstelbloem and A. Meijer (eds.), *Migration and the New Technological Borders of Europe*. Basingstoke, UK: Palgrave Macmillan.

Foucault, M. 2003. *"Society Must Be Defended". Lectures at the Collège de France, 1975–76*, tr. D. Macey. New York: Picador.

Gellner, E. 1983. *Nations and Nationalism*. Ithaca, NY: Cornell University Press.

LGBTQI Refugees GR. 2017. Twitter. 21 May. https://twitter.com/LGBTQIRefugeeGR/status/866328188963737600/photo/1 (Accessed 26 November 2017).

Snyder, T. 2005. "The Wall Around the West". *Eurozine*. http://www.eurozine.com/articles/2005-01-06-snyder-en.html (Accessed 7 January 2016).

CHAPTER 2

"Migrants" vis-à-vis "Refugees": Towards a "Rationalisation" of Migration Control and Management

Abstract Since summer 2015 and the wave of mass migration, the dominant political discourse systematically attempts to consolidate anew a crucial dichotomy between "migrants" and "refugees". This chapter focuses on this dichotomy that is actually linked to specific EU preconditions and criteria. The aim of this chapter is to uncover the concomitant "rationalisation" of migration control and management that is in direct correlation with this dichotomy and, consequently, with the construction of migrants' identity and their future within Western societies.

Keywords Migrants • Refugees • Borders • Asylum • Migration control

"The twenty-first century will be the century of the migrant not only because of the record number of migrants today but also because this is the century in which all previous forms of social expulsion and migratory resistance have reemerged and become more active than ever before" (Nail 2015: 7). The above quote by Thomas Nail summarises aptly the situation we are witnessing at the beginning of the twenty-first century, when the so-called migration flows[1] have literally reached an unprecedented

[1] At this point, it should be highlighted that the term "migration flows", which has dominated the public discourse during the last years, is quite revealing of the dominant way of thinking regarding migrants. Of course, as it is rightly underlined, "[t]he fluid and turbulent

T. Lagios et al., *Borders, Bodies and Narratives of Crisis in Europe*,
https://doi.org/10.1007/978-3-319-75586-1_2

peak.[2] At the same time, our epoch has been described as "a time of the triumph of borders, an epoch of border fetishism" (Khosravi 2010: 1). Undoubtedly, these borders do not function in the same ways and with the same consequences for all people, despite the fact that their incessant diffusion, as we are going to highlight in the following, tends to apply to a steadily growing number of people.[3] For, although a small, privileged minority seems to live, work and travel in a so-called borderless world, "it has become increasingly evident that for a large majority, borders are not only being reinforced, but are being redrawn in ways that determine rights of citizenship and even more profoundly, the very 'borders' of what constitutes 'humanity' itself" (Harper and Raman 2008: 4–5).

Within this frame, since summer 2015, the dominant political discourse has systematically attempted to consolidate anew a crucial dichotomy; the dichotomy between "migrants" and "refugees". Besides, "[t]he current international framework addressing international mobility is based on the distinction between 'refugees' and 'migrants'" (Scalettaris 2010: 252). On the one hand, "migrants" are, in essence, represented as "illegal migrants", whose attempt to enter the Western world is regarded as unnecessary and, thus, as *a priori* condemnable and rejected. Actually, the term "illegal migrant" itself is a product of both legal and moral connotations (Dauvergne 2008; Kirkwood et al. 2016), whereas it is a *par excellence* Euro- and

force of migration is not a new discovery. Societies have always feared the turbulence and irregular movement of migrants and have described them in the same fluid terms" (Nail 2015: 224). Within this frame, twenty-first-century "migration flows", represented as "flooding" the European space, appear to crystallise the properties of liquids. More specifically, the fact that liquids always acquire the shape of the space they take up or through which they move, as well as the fact that no segmentation is observed in liquids when external forces are exercised; on the contrary, they flow continuously. Migrants' representation as "liquids" and "flows" has not been restricted exclusively to a symbolic and rhetorical level; European border politics has literally treated migrants as "flows". "Migration flows" are directed through particular pathways, changing direction or becoming blocked like a liquid flow, whereas migrants, having lost their human substance, are becoming a liquid mass, perpetually in motion.

[2] It is estimated that around 75 million people across the world are today in a position of a so-called forced displacement for several reasons (Agier 2016).

[3] We should keep in mind that, within a rapidly globalised world, there is noted a significant rise in human mobility, in general; even those, who consider themselves "invulnerable" to dichotomies and tend to regard migrants as "dangerous" and "miasmatic" Others are quite often obliged to constantly move for business, and so on. On the new conditions of globalisation and mobility in Western societies, see Cresswell (2006); Sassen (1996).

Western-centric term, since the "illegal" entry is always referring to Western borders (Besters and Brom 2010). On the other hand, "refugees" have at least the chance to have their applications for asylum examined. So, it should not be considered as accidental that, within the frame of these new dichotomies and evaluations regarding the worth of human life itself, Croatia, Serbia and the FYR of Macedonia decided to close their borders to every migrant not coming from Syria, Iraq and Afghanistan, during the night of 18 November 2015 (Amnesty International 2015). It was a decision depriving a great number of people of the right to apply for asylum and the opportunity to claim the supposedly international human rights; the only criterion for this arbitrary decision was migrants' nationality. Following the building of fences by Hungary and Slovenia, the FYR of Macedonia announced the building of a fence along its borders with Greece, as well. As a result, thousands of migrants from Iran, Bangladesh, Morocco, Algeria and elsewhere were trapped for days along the Greece-FYR of Macedonia border, under literally miserable conditions. Some decided to go on hunger strike, sew their lips and write slogans on their bodies, ending up sitting obstinately in front of the border guards to remind the Western world of their presence there. So, how has this new condition of "selective" borders been established? Under which circumstances have we become witnesses of the construction of fences and of borders' opening and closing, defining whose life is worth more?

During the last years, the term "illegal migrant", despite its obvious Western-centric signification, and its correlation with the rhetoric and practices of the extreme right,[4] has literally intruded into the public sphere and discourse: from the newspapers' front pages and politicians' speeches to scientific studies, even school books.[5] As it is rightly asserted, "[n]ever before in history has such a large group of people being labeled as 'illegal

[4] This has been exactly the rhetoric used by the Golden Dawn, the Greek ultranationalist extreme right party, leading to a series of murderous attacks against migrants that culminated in the murder of the 34-year-old anti-fascist musician Pavlos Fyssas, on 18 September 2013. Unfortunately, the racist attacks are still continuing, whereas in the (September) 2015 national elections the Golden Dawn won 6.2% of election vote.

[5] An indicative example is the History textbook for the 3rd Grade of General Lyceum (High School), in Greece. The book's writers reproduce the dominant xenophobic views, attributing to "illegal migrants" the rise of criminality and the consequent insecurity of the Greek citizens: "[...] the sudden and uncontrolled rise of illegal migrants and economic migrants are creating serious problems of security to the Greek society" (Givalos et al. 2010: 200).

people' in this way" (Nail 2015: 200). Even though there has been noted a considerable post-War problematisation and consequent criminalisation of "illegal migrants",[6] representing them often as "law breakers", "job takers" and "public burdens" (Inda 2006), that culminated, for several reasons, after the 1970s advent of neoliberalism,[7] since spring 2015, the term "illegal migrant" has been, to an extent, re-invented and has dynamically re-appeared in the forefront vis-à-vis the term "refugee".

According to the United Nations "1951 Convention Relating to the Status of Refugees", grounded on article 14 of the 1948 "Universal Declaration of Human Rights" and still in force today, every person who "owing to well-founded fear of being persecuted for reasons of race, religion, nationality, membership of a particular social group or political opinion, is outside the country of his nationality and is unable or, owing to such fear, is unwilling to avail himself of the protection of that country; or who, not having a nationality and being outside the country of his former habitual residence as a result of such events, is unable or, owing to such fear, is unwilling to return to it" is considered a refugee (UNHCR 2010: 14). But, even before the formal recognition of the status of the "refugee", refugees as a mass phenomenon had already made their dynamic appearance at the end of World War I within the new territorial structures created after the peace treaties (Agamben 1995); for example, Greece experienced the first mass movement of refugees—around 1,200,000, in autumn 1922—following the Greco-Turkish War of 1919–1922. Nonetheless, during the last two years, as an aftermath of the war in Syria,[8] the term "refugee" has made a spectacular re-entry into the dominant rhetoric and practices of EU migration politics, as well as into the public discourse, to characterise specific national groups.

[6] It should not be considered as accidental that we now speak of "Crimmigration Law"; namely, the institutionalisation of laws on migration that proceed to a conjunction of migratory and penal legislation (Stumpf 2013). A typical example has been, among others, the Greek legislation on migration (Baldwin-Edwards 2009; Sitaropoulos 2000). Also, for an interesting analysis of the dominant metaphors in legal texts on migration, see Cunningham-Parmeter (2011).

[7] As it has been rightly asserted by C. Cantat, "with the start of the economic depression in the 1970s, followed by the fall of the Soviet Union, migrants became key figures of difference against which people of the EU member states could be argued to share a common 'Europeanity'" (2015: 16).

[8] According to the United Nations High Commissioner for Refugees (UNHCR), more than one million people arrived to Europe by sea in 2015. Specifically, more than 850,000 migrants, primarily from Syria, Afghanistan and Iraq, reached the Greek shores (UNHCR 2016; Council of Europe 2017).

Undoubtedly, it is not just about an innocent game and exchange of signifiers. Nor has it been born within the frame of an unprecedented historical context. For, refugees did not appear for the first time two years ago, as an aftermath of the war in Syria. During the last years, several countries, such as Iraq, Afghanistan and Somalia, have suffered from bloody wars that forced great parts of their populations to apply for asylum in another country. Quite characteristic of the pretentious rationale that dictates this dichotomy between refugees and migrants is the fact that Serbia and the FYR of Macedonia decided, in February 2016, to exclude Afghanis, as well, from those who could cross their borders—of course, the condition in Afghanistan had not changed in the least. Simultaneously, several countries—among others, Slovenia, Croatia, Serbia and the FYR of Macedonia—announced restrictions to the number of daily entries of refugees. From this perspective, the spectacular re-entry of the term "refugee" vis-à-vis the term "migrant" has, in fact, marked a decisive change in EU migration politics. This, methodically constructed and consolidated, dichotomy between "refugees" and "migrants" has reinforced a series of migration control mechanisms, introducing clear hierarchies and evaluative judgments, since such demarcation lines, delimitations and restrictions "not only produce the domain of intelligible bodies, but produce as well a domain of unthinkable, abject, unlivable bodies" (Butler 1993: xi). Furthermore, we should take into consideration that even during the short period of "open" European borders, in summer 2015, migrants' camps kept, in fact, operating; for, "[s]ince the early 1970s when the figure of the 'illegal' migrant acquired a global prominence, there has been proliferation and diversification of such spaces" (Mezzadra and Neilson 2013: 147). So, these spaces kept working behind the scenes to confine and exclude all those who kept carrying the deadly stamp of the "(illegal) migrant", those "wretched of the earth", the "bare lives" of contemporary Western societies.

As a result, for every "refugee", who, by risking his/her life, succeeds in arriving to Europe, there are hundreds of thousands of confined "illegal migrants" in camps and detention centres all over the world. Within this frame, Turkey has constituted an essential part in migrants' filtering procedures with camps and other facilities, but also a main centre for their relocation.[9] It is indicative that the "Facility for Refugees in Turkey" has

[9] Besides, the process of relocation plays an extremely significant part in European migration politics. As Jean-Claude Juncker stated on 13 September 2017: "People who have no right to stay in Europe must be returned to their countries of origin. When only 36% of irregular migrants are returned, it is clear we need to significantly step up our work" (European Commission 2017a).

managed €3 billion for 2016 and 2017, in order to address refugees' needs in Turkey, with an emphasis on "humanitarian assistance, education, migration management, health, municipal infrastructure, and socio-economic support" (European Commission 2016).[10] Accordingly, the EU has provided important financial assistance for the Turkish Coast Guard, in order to prevent migrants from entering Greece. For this purpose, Turkey is in close co-operation with the Greek Coast Guard and the Greek authorities to strengthen the control and surveillance mechanisms, under the umbrella of Frontières Extérieures (FRONTEX) that operates in the Aegean Sea since 2009. FRONTEX, an EU agency for border control established in 2004, has as its declared objective to ensure "the free movement of persons within the European Union" and to transform the European territory into an "area of freedom, security and justice" (European Union 2004: 1).[11] Paradoxically, this humanist "vision" excludes certain human beings…

For, it is in the name of this freedom, security and justice "for all" that there are already functioning in several countries the so-called hotspots—among others, in Greece[12] and Italy. According to the EU Hotspot Approach, hotspots are centres for the identification, registration and fingerprinting of incoming migrants by each member-state, in close co-operation with FRONTEX, European Asylum Support Office (EASO) and European Police Office (EUROPOL), as well as with Eurojust and European Maritime Safety Agency (EMSA) (European Commission 2014); the data of the recording process are registered in the European database EURODAC, to which we are going to refer more extensively in Chap. 5. It was for this purpose that Jean-Claude Juncker, president of the European Commission, rather cynically stated in October 2015: "I want to be clear: people must be registered. No registration, no rights"

[10] And, in March 2017, the EU launched a €34 million Conditional Cash Transfer Programme, in order to enable around 230,000 refugee children to attend school in Turkey (European Commission 2017b).

[11] For a brief presentation of the structure and operation of FRONTEX, see also Kasparek (2010).

[12] In November 2017, five hotspots are in operation in Greece; more specifically, on the Aegean islands of Lesvos, Chios, Samos, Leros and Kos (European Commission 2017c). The recent law on migration, passed on 3 April 2016 by the Greek parliament, put a special emphasis on the facilities, function and staffing of hotspots and other centres for migrants' identification and recording (Law 4375/2016).

(European Commission 2015).[13] But, even if migrants succeed in passing these first filtering stages, a series of new, even more refined filters is waiting for them at the core of the European territory. It is indicative that, in September 2015, the German government proceeded to the foundation of similar centres for migrants' identification—initially, in Manching and Bamberg in Bayern (Auer 2015; *Welt* 2015). These so-called Balkanzentrum were destined for those who had already passed former control procedures in a Balkan country and applied for asylum in Germany. The target was the, as quickly as possible, examination of each "case" and the preparation for its relocation.

Hence, migrants' humiliation and depreciation do not end either with the acceptance of their admission into a European, "civilised" country or with the consequent examination of their application for asylum; for, "[d]espite the 'human' in human rights, being merely human is not enough to ensure legal standing in many instances" (Dauvergne 2008: 21). Nonetheless, even in the cases of those "refugees" whose lives are deemed as "worthy of life", there are still prevailing specific stereotypes and representations regarding the identity of the "refugee" who "deserves" to be granted asylum within Western societies.[14] These stereotypes and representations predetermine and define, to a great extent, the result of the whole asylum procedure and, consequently, migrants' "future". For, everyone who claims the "refugee" status is expected to fully perform his/her identity as a refugee, confirming, justifying and legitimising not only the granting of asylum *per se*, but also the measures taken for dealing with the "humanist crisis", as well as the tears effortlessly shed for the "refugee drama" by those who have so violently bred it with their political and economic decisions on a global scale. As Khosravi underlines, "pain and suffering have become the hallmarks of refugeeness. The term 'refugee' generally signifies deprived and underprivileged people. A 'real' refugee is thus supposed to be a 'profound', 'poor', 'traumatized', 'serious' and of course 'sad' person. [...]. Refugees have to perform 'refugeeness'" (2010: 73). Therefore, migrants' future within Western societies will be judged

[13] Regarding his statement "No registration: no rights", Juncker also commented on his Twitter account: "Truly, I am Europe's progressive voice on migration" (2015).

[14] These dominant stereotypes regarding non-Western nations have, usually, little to do with the culture and the distinct characteristics of these nations. As Said rightly highlights: "Orientalism is – and does not simply represent – a considerable dimension of modern political-intellectual culture, and as such has less to do with the Orient than it does with 'our' world" (1977: 12).

and decided according to the successful performance of the refugee's role and identity; but, it is a future that is, in fact, already prefixed and predetermined based exactly upon this very identity.

Thus, a series of new mechanisms of migration control and management and, consequently, migrants' admittance into the Western world has been recently established. As we are going to see analytically in the next chapter, these mechanisms are linked to specific preconditions and clearly defined criteria established by EU member-states, such as educational level and class; what is called "migration management is fundamentally about making migration economically beneficial, [...]" (Geiger and Pécoud 2010: 14). However, these criteria, connected with the function of the labour market and the neoliberal values of competition and productivity, are systematically concealed behind the dominant dichotomy between "migrants" and "refugees". For, are there really any criteria—for example, belonging to racial, sexual or religious minorities under persecution, economic reasons or ongoing war—that can actually define whose life is really in danger and is worth to be granted asylum? In other words, how is it even thinkable to categorise and evaluate one's life according to his/her country of origin or other established "criteria"? How is it possible to articulate evaluative judgements regarding human life *per se*? Nonetheless, it is within the frame of this dichotomy and these largely arbitrary and paradoxical criteria that only those who are going to be labelled as "refugees" will have the chance to move, even for some kilometres, within the European territory; of course, thanks to their "special", desired characteristics and qualities, and provided that they would have succeeded in passing the deadly passage of the Aegean Sea or some other itinerary. On the contrary, all those who are going to be labeled as "(illegal) migrants" – that is, the overwhelming majority—will be deported, remain confined in a camp or hotspot in southern Europe, Turkey or elsewhere, or try to discover another "illegal" passage to Europe, which, of course, will make their journey even more dangerous.[15] Therefore, according to this rationale, "[t]o be 'illegal' is thus to be fundamentally an improper subject", an "anti-citizen" (Inda 2006:

[15] It is a fact that the new control mechanisms do continuously block and reduce these "illegal" passages. And, as long as these passages are getting fewer and fewer and as long as the surveillance mechanisms are intensified, the number of migrants who cannot survive their journey is steadily rising. According to some estimates, for every migrant's dead body found at the coast line of the "developed" world, at least two more deaths are not recorded, whereas one out of four persons has perished during the journey to Europe (Brian and Laczko 2014; Spijkerboer 2007; Grant 2011).

109–110). Within this context, the re-invention of the dichotomy between "migrants" and "refugees" marks the rationalisation of a nexus of power relations that control, categorise, confine and redistribute migrants along an expanded borderline that is not restricted exclusively to every single part within the European territory, but is now extending to North Africa and the Middle East. And, this supposed "rational" filtering does, actually, reinforce the precariousness of migrants' life; the thousands of deaths along borders, as well as along the various passages to Europe; the racist and xenophobic attacks against migrants in many European cities; police's brutal violence against them; their desperate hunger strikes and even suicides in camps and hotspots within totally unlivable conditions, as we are going to see in Chap. 4. For, even in those cases where there are issued fervent declarations in favour of the opposite,[16] the target remains the invention and consolidation of more flexible and efficient mechanisms of migrants' illegalisation, criminalisation and repression, their exclusion and depreciation, and, when necessary, their exploitation.

References

Agamben, G. 1995. "We Refugees". *Symposium: A Quarterly Journal in Modern Literature*, 49(2): 114–119.

Agier, M. 2016. *Borderlands: Towards an Anthropology of the Cosmopolitan Condition*, tr. D. Fernbach. Malden, MA: Polity Press.

Amnesty International. 2015. "Refugee Crisis: Balkans Border Blocks Leave Thousands Stranded", 20 November. https://www.amnesty.org/en/latest/news/2015/11/refugee-crisis-balkans-border-blocks-leave-thousands-segregated-and-stranded-in-greece/ (Accessed 22 November 2017).

Auer, K. 2015. "Bamberg hat den Platz – theoretisch". *Süddeutsche Zeitung*, 6 November. http://www.sueddeutsche.de/bayern/registrierzentrum-fuer-fluechtlinge-bamberg-hat-den-platz-theoretisch-1.2725042 (Accessed 8 November 2015).

Baldwin-Edwards, M. 2009. "Greece". In M. Baldwin-Edwards and A. Kraler (eds.), *Regine. Regularisations in Europe*. Amsterdam: European Commission/Amsterdam University Press.

[16] Quite characteristically, on 28 June 2017, Parliamentary Assembly of the Council of Europe (PACE) has called for an end to the "negative rhetoric" about migrants, since "ungrounded fears" have enabled some politicians and media to present "a distorted image of migration as a threat". Of course, according to PACE, this is deemed as necessary, since migration can potentially contribute to Europe's "economic growth, demographic renewal and cultural diversity" (2017).

Besters, M. and Brom, F.W.A. 2010. "'Greedy' Information Technology: The Digitalization of the European Migration Policy". *European Journal of Migration and Law*, 12: 455–470. https://doi.org/10.1163/157181610X535782.

Brian, T. and Laczko, F. 2014. "Counting Migrant Deaths: An International Overview". In T. Brian and F. Laczko (eds.), *Fatal Journeys. Tracking Lives Lost during Migration*. Geneva: International Organization for Migration.

Butler, J. 1993. *Bodies That Matter. On the Discursive Limits of "Sex"*. New York/London: Routledge.

Cantat, C. 2015. "Narratives and Counter-narratives of Europe. Constructing and Contesting Europeanity". *Cahiers Mémoire et Politique*, 3: 5–30. https://www.academia.edu/27203857/Narratives_and_counter-narratives_of_Europe._Constructing_and_contesting_Europeanity (Accessed 24 October 2017).

Council of Europe. 2017. "Report to the Greek Government on the Visits to Greece Carried Out by the European Committee for the Prevention of Torture and Inhuman or Degrading Treatment or Punishment (CPT) from 13 to 18 April and 19 to 25 July 2016", 26 September. http://www.politico.eu/wp-content/uploads/2017/09/CPT-report.pdf (Accessed 30 October 2017).

Cresswell, T. 2006. *On the Move. Mobility in the Modern Western World*. London/New York: Routledge.

Cunningham-Parmeter, K. 2011. "Alien Language: Immigration Metaphors and the Jurisprudence of Otherness". *Fordham Law Review*, 79(4): 1545–1598. http://ir.lawnet.fordham.edu/flr/vol79/iss4/5 (Accessed 23 November 2017).

Dauvergne, C. 2008. *Making People Illegal. What Globalization Means for Migration and Law*. New York: Cambridge University Press.

European Commission. 2014. "Glossary for the European Agenda on Migration". https://ec.europa.eu/home-affairs/sites/homeaffairs/files/what-we-do/policies/european-agenda-migration/background-information/docs/glossary_for_the_european_agenda_on_migration_en.pdf (Accessed 7 October 2017).

European Commission. 2015. "Speaking Points of President Juncker – Press Conference on Western Balkans Route Leaders' Meeting", 26 October. http://europa.eu/rapid/press-release_SPEECH-15-5905_el.htm (Accessed 12 December 2017).

European Commission. 2016. "Fact Sheet: Managing the Refugee Crisis, EU-Turkey Statement", 4 October. http://europa.eu/rapid/press-release_MEMO-16-3218_en.htm (Accessed 7 October 2017).

European Commission. 2017a. "Towards an Efficient and Credible EU Return Policy". https://ec.europa.eu/home-affairs/sites/homeaffairs/files/what-we-do/policies/european-agenda-migration/20170927_factsheet_towards_an_efficient_and_credible_eu_return_policy_en.pdf (Accessed 8 October 2017).

European Commission. 2017b. "Press Release: EU Increases Humanitarian aid Budget for Education of Children in Emergencies", 20 September. http://europa.eu/rapid/press-release_IP-17-3273_en.htm (Accessed 7 October 2017).

European Commission. 2017c. "Hotspot State of Play", 27 November. https://ec.europa.eu/home-affairs/sites/homeaffairs/files/what-we-do/policies/european-agenda-migration/press-material/docs/state_of_play_-_hotspots_en.pdf (Accessed 7 October 2017).

European Union. 2004. "Council Regulation (EC) No 2007/2004 of 26 October 2004 establishing a European Agency for the Management of Operational Cooperation at the External Borders of the Member States of the European Union". *Official Journal of the European Union*, 25 November. http://frontex.europa.eu/assets/About_Frontex/frontex_regulation_en.pdf (Accessed 13 January 2016).

Geiger, M. and Pécoud, A. 2010. "The Politics of International Migration Management". In M. Geiger and A. Pécoud (eds.), *The Politics of International Migration Management*. Basingstoke, UK: Palgrave Macmillan.

Givalos, M., Grigroropoulou, V., Kotroyiannos, D., and Maniatis, G. 2010. *History of Social Sciences. Student Book, 3rd Grade, General Lyceum* [in Greek]. Athens: School Book Publishing Organization (OEBD).

Grant, S. 2011. "Recording and Identifying European Frontier Deaths". *European Journal of Migration and Law*, 13: 135–156. https://doi.org/10.1163/157181611X571259.

Harper, I. and Raman, P. 2008. "Less than Human? Diaspora, Disease and the Question of Citizenship". *International Migration*, 46(5): 3–26. https://doi.org/10.1111/j.1468-2435.2008.00486.x.

Inda, J.X. 2006. *Targeting Immigrants. Government, Technology, and Ethics*. Malden, MA: Blackwell Publishing.

Juncker, J.-C. 2015. Twitter, 25 October. https://twitter.com/juncker_jc/status/658427389576388608 (Accessed 27 October 2015).

Kasparek, B. 2010. "Borders and Populations in Flux: Frontex's Place in the European Union's Migration Management". In M. Geiger and A. Pécoud (eds.), *The Politics of International Migration Management*. Basingstoke. UK: Palgrave Macmillan.

Khosravi, S. 2010. *'Illegal Traveller'. An Auto-Ethnography of Borders*. Basingstoke, UK: Palgrave Macmillan.

Kirkwood, S., Goodman, S., McVittie, C., and McKinlay, A. 2016. *The Language of Asylum. Refugees and Discourse*. Basingstoke, UK: Palgrave Macmillan.

Law 4375/2016. "Organisation and function of the Asylum Service, Appeals Authority, Reception and Identification Service, constitution of the General Secretariat for Reception, adaptation of the Greek Legislation to the provisions of the Directive 2013/32/EU of the European Parliament and Council 'on common procedures for granting and withdrawing international protection (recast)' (L 180/29.6.2013), provisions for the labour of beneficiaries of international protection and other provisions" [in Greek]. *Government Gazette*, 3 April. https://www.synigoros.gr/resources/docs/n-4375-2016.pdf (Accessed 12 October 2017).

Mezzadra, S. and Neilson, B. 2013. *Border as Method, or, the Multiplication of Labour*. Durham/London: Duke University Press.
Nail, T. 2015. *The Figure of the Migrant*. Stanford, CA: Stanford University Press.
PACE. 2017. "Call for an End to 'Negative Rhetoric' on Migrants". http://www.assembly.coe.int/nw/xml/News/News-View-EN.asp?newsid=6719&lang=2&cat=8 (Accessed 7 October 2017).
Said, E.W. 1977. *Orientalism*. London/New York: Penguin Books.
Sassen, S. 1996. *Losing Control? Sovereignty in an Age of Globalization*. New York: Columbia University Press.
Scalettaris, G. 2010. "Refugees or Migrants? The UNHCR's Comprehensive Approach to Afghan Mobility into Iran and Pakistan". In M. Geiger and A. Pécoud (eds.), *The Politics of International Migration Management*. Basingstoke, UK: Palgrave Macmillan.
Sitaropoulos, N. 2000. "Modern Greek Asylum Policy and Practice in the Context of the Relevant European Developments". *Journal of Refugee Studies*, 13(1): 105–117.
Spijkerboer, T. 2007. "The Human Costs of Border Control". *European Journal of Migration and Law*, 9: 127–139. https://doi.org/10.1163/138836407X179337.
Stumpf, J.P. 2013. "The Process Is the Punishment in Crimmigration Law". In K.F. Aas and M. Bosworth (eds.), *The Borders of Punishment. Migration, Citizenship, and Social Exclusion*. New York: Oxford University Press.
UNHCR. 2010. "Convention and Protocol Relating to the Status of Refugees". http://www.unhcr.org/3b66c2aa10 (Accessed 7 October 2017).
UNHCR. 2016. "Global Trends. Forced Displacement in 2015". http://www.unhcr.org/576408cd7.pdf (Accessed 25 November 2017).
Welt. 2015. "Bayern zufrieden mit 'Balkanzentrum' in Manching", 16 September. http://www.welt.de/regionales/bayern/article146484530/Bayern-zufrieden-mit-Balkanzentrum-in-Manching.html (Accessed 21 September 2015).

CHAPTER 3

Opening and Closing Borders: Capitalism Is Speeding Up

Abstract This chapter focuses on the recent transformations of migration management; namely, on the transition from migrants' exclusion to refugees' temporary acceptance as a useful labour force in several European countries. The impermanent opening of the European borders in 2015 led to the conditional acceptance of a number of refugees, aiming at their exploitation as another gear of capitalism. As we attempt to highlight, it is the most qualified and disciplined bodies that have the "chance" to settle and work in central and northern capitalist Europe, after a long process of evaluation and classification of their own subjectivity.

Keywords Capitalism • Labour force • Migrants' exploitation • Borders

"It was my good fortune to be deported to Auschwitz only in 1944, that is, after the German government had decided, because of the growing scarcity of labor, to lengthen the average life span of the prisoners destined for elimination; [...]" (Levi 2015: 55). Comparing himself with all those who did not manage to survive, Primo Levi regarded as sheer "luck" the fact that he escaped the gas chambers in exchange for his labour force that became the object of a cruel and merciless exploitation within the barbarous conditions of Auschwitz concentration camp. However, in his attempt to describe, as

T. Lagios et al., *Borders, Bodies and Narratives of Crisis in Europe*, https://doi.org/10.1007/978-3-319-75586-1_3

eloquently as possible, the humiliation and degradation that he and his cellmates were experiencing in the camp, he continued writing: "It's not possible to sink lower than this; no human condition more wretched exists, nor could it be imagined" (ibid: 73). For, even death does not constitute a univocal concept and does not refer exclusively to biological death; even though, through the intensifying medicalisation, it is this dimension of death that is dominating in Western societies, transforming death into the "absolute evil" in our civilisation. Nevertheless, death, except for its biological dimension, might actually consist in social and political death, exclusion and rejection, human life's depreciation and humiliation, condemnation to mere survival and consequent abjection (Foucault 2003). As Hannah Arendt remarked, "[b]rought up in the conviction that life is the highest good and death the greatest dismay, we became witnesses and victims of worse terrors than death [...]" (1994: 112). So, neither life, nor death, but condemnation to survival in wholly unlivable conditions; eventually, this seems to be at stake within the frame of a biopolitical power that focuses on the enhancement and preservation of those lives deemed as "worthy of life", and the dissolution and depreciation of all others.[1] Through this prism, taking into consideration the aforementioned distinction between "refugees" and "migrants", that is, "the heuristic value of the distinction between skilled and unskilled migration" (Mezzadra and Neilson 2013: 132), how could we actually re-read and evaluate the following events?

In August and September 2015, thousands of migrants arrived at the Munich central railway station; the majority came from Syria (Connolly 2015; Hengst and Sperber 2015). Hundreds of people welcomed the Syrian refugees, by applauding and singing. They offered them water and food, as well as gifts and toys to the children, whereas smiling policemen were giving them directions and necessary information. At the same time, journalists from all over the world were recording the event with their cameras. Refugees were standing with awe and responding to this hospitality by shouting loudly "Germany-Germany". Their voices were resonating in the station as a sign of their gratitude to the "hospitality" of the German nation. It was *the* moment of the triumph of Western civilisation and humanist values. But was it, indeed, an act of hospitality, let alone of

[1] In Agamben's words: "[...] no longer either *to make die* or *to make live*, but *to make survive*. The decisive activity of biopower in our time consists in the production not of life or death, but rather of a mutable and virtually infinite survival" (1999: 155; emphasis in the original).

"unconditional hospitality"? Could we, actually, consider it as a form of "unconditional hospitality" *per se*,[2] within the frame of neoliberal societies that are grounded on economic efficiency and political claims, but, equally, on the invocation of exceptions (Ong 2006) and the consolidation of dichotomies, such as the one between migrants and refugees?

Almost six months before this impermanent "opening" of the borders, a scientific study by *Bertelsmann Stiftung* appeared in the forefront, on 27 March 2015; *Bertelsmann Stiftung* is an independent private foundation, founded in 1977, which is well-known for its neoliberal orientation. So, what did this study claim and how could it be related to the function and the recent opening and closing of the European borders? *Bertelsmann Stiftung*'s study attempted to legitimise, with its scientific prestige and its supposedly "impartial" analysis, a series of discussions that had started some time ago within the EU. The study proceeded to the assessment of future population figures and labour-force participation rates by age and gender, developing several scenarios based upon these parameters. According to one such scenario, birth deficit in Germany, along with other demographic rates, is expected to reduce the potential labour force from 45 million people today to below 29 million people by 2050 (Fuchs et al. 2015). And, even if the German government decided to adopt a "retirement at 70" policy, this would result in an additional potential of just about 3 million employed persons in 2035 and another 2.5 million people in 2050. According to the study's findings, the only solution to deal with this demanding problem of the German economy is, in essence, the exploitation of migrants' labour. But, here, the following issue arises: since most east-European economies seem to gradually exit the financial crisis and migration from EU states will generally decline in the relatively near future, Germany cannot count on them for the future supply of labour force. According to Jörg Dräger, member of the Executive Board of *Bertelsmann Stiftung*, "Germany cannot rely on continued high immigra-

[2] In fact, the question is if there could be any form of "unconditional hospitality", given that any kind of hospitality does presuppose and involve a degree of hostility in juxtaposition with the sentiment of hospitality that supposedly inheres at the heart of any act of hospitality. Derrida, following Benveniste's etymology, remarks that the word "hospitalité" originates from the Latin word "hostis" that means the foreigner who can be welcomed as either enemy or guest (Derrida and Dufourmantelle 2000). Nonetheless, even though "unconditional hospitality" may appear as an almost impossible act, this does, in no way, imply, for Derrida, that we should resign from it; on the contrary, from an ethical viewpoint, we should try for the impossible.

tion from within the European Union. We must set a course now that makes Germany more attractive as a destination country for third-country nationals as well" (Bertelsmann Stiftung 2015). So, there is emerging an imperative need for migration from the so-called third countries; it is estimated that within the next 36 years, an annual average of between 276,000 and 491,000 people must arrive from third countries, in order for the potential labour force to be maintained at a constant level (Fuchs et al. 2015). Thus, the above findings could be translated as follows: the German government should consider changing its migration policy; namely, opening, under specific conditions, its borders to people outside the EU and offering them an "attractive" environment for their smooth acclimatisation as a potential labour force.

In order to further clarify the multileveled dimensions of this study, we should read it in juxtaposition with several statements and analyses by politicians, academics and technocrats, during 2015. For example, Patrick Artus, economist and director of research and studies at the French bank Natixis, in a memo in September 2015, assessed that refugees' reception could offer to Europe the chance "not only to honor its position as a democratic Union that is wealthy and respectful of tradition, but also to expand its growth prospects" (cited in De Martino 2015). On the same wavelength, with an equally sincere and honest interest in the continuation of the European Union's democratic tradition, Holger Schmieding, Chief Economist at Berenberg Bank, estimated that refugees' reception could have positive short- and long-term economic benefits to European economies (2015), whereas Emmanuelle Auriol, professor of economics at the University of Toulouse, underlined that "[i]n general, refugees are young, in good health, with a desire to work. They bring back more [money] than they cost" (*RTBF* 2015). Even more cynical appeared M. Fratzscher, president of the "German Institute for Economic Research" ("Deutsches Institut für Wirtschaftsforschung", DIW), and S. Junker, Deputy Head of Department of Forecasting and Economic Policy at DIW, who both stressed that "integration is still an investment that will pay off in the long run" (2015: 616).

In favour of the above opinions concerning refugees' integration have also been many, rather profitable, European industries. During the last two years, most economists have, in fact, agreed with each other about refugees' possible benefits to European economies and their potentially significant contribution to the confrontation of the shortage of specialised, skilled labour.[3] Among others, in October 2015, Tom Enders, chief executive of Airbus, claimed that Germany should follow the example of the USA and proceed to the liberation of the labour market for the creation of more, low-paid jobs for refugees and their faster and smoother integration into society (*Süddeutsche Zeitung* 2015). In the same direction, Siemens AG introduced a multi-stage, long-term programme for integrating refugees, in September 2015, providing donations and practical support worth a total of €2 million, whereas special training classes for refugees, including German language courses, were planned at the company's various locations all over Germany. According to Janina Kugel, head of Human Resources at Siemens, "[t]hrough our European training program that we started in 2012, we've gained valuable experience in the training of young people from other countries. We can now make use of this experience to prepare refugees with suitable prior qualifications for their careers" (Siemens AG 2015). From its side, Badische Anilin und Soda Fabrik (BASF), one of the largest chemical producers in the world, also started a series of programmes for refugees' incorporation in 2015 (BASF 2015), while Dieter Zetsche, head of DAIMLER, stated that "[m]ost of the refugees are young, well trained and highly motivated. That's exactly the sort of person we're looking for" (cited in Zimmermann 2015).

As one might have expected, this is the EU official rhetoric, as well. It is quite characteristic that migrants' labour and their integration into the European labour market has been an issue of systematic concern during the last years, especially after the 2015 wave of mass migration. More specifically, in January 2016, the European Commission published the evaluation of a 2014 survey, entitled "How are refugees faring on the labour market in Europe?", whereas in March 2016, the study for the Committee on Employment and Social Affairs (EMPL) of the European Parliament, entitled "Labour Market Integration of Refugees: Strategies and good practices, was published". The first study explicitly underlines that its main target is "to improve the integration of refugees and other migrants and support their economic and social contribution to the EU"

[3] Of course, these references to refugees as skilled, specialised labour are, in no case, arbitrary or coincidental. Quite indicative has been a survey by UNHCR, published in June 2015. According to the survey's findings, covering the period 1 April 2015–31 May 2015, in a total of 670 refugees from Syria, who answered the questionnaire—on the whole, during this period 18,257 Syrian refugees arrived at the Greek borders—39.7% (266 persons) had a university degree and 45.67% (306 persons) a high-school diploma, having considerable professional skills and qualifications (UNHCR 2015).

(European Commission 2016: 31), examining several aspects of migrants' employment, such as the employment rate for women.[4] It is very interesting that an emphasis is put upon the distinction between "low-", "medium-" and "high-skilled" refugees, reinforcing the distinction between (skilled) "refugees" and (unskilled) "migrants", with refugees being represented as "overqualified than other migrants" (ibid: 6). Accordingly, the second study aims at evaluating European strategies and enabling member-states to support refugees' integration, underlining that "[i]ntegration remains primarily a national competence and the implementation of integration policies falls under the responsibility of the Member States" (European Parliament 2016: 12). So, it turns out that "a relation between labor time, wage, and borders is essential to the construction of a national labor market" (Mezzadra and Neilson 2013: 134), even though "nation-state sovereignty is challenged by global movements of capital" (Brown 2010: 22) and, consequently, as we are going to see in the next chapter, by the new mechanisms of border control, security and militarisation.

Within this frame, on 20 June 2017, Commissioners D. Avramopoulos and M. Thyssen chose the World Refugee Day to announce the launch of the EU Skills Profile Tool for non-EU citizens. As Avramopoulos highlighted, "[m]igration is not just about challenges, it is also about opportunities. Refugees and migrants come with their own experiences, talents and skills. These can be real assets for our economies and societies overall" (European Commission 2017a: 1). For this purpose, the EU Skills Profile Tool is about the recording and assessment of migrants' qualifications and working experiences, so as to be integrated into the European labour market and contribute to the growth of European businesses and economies; of course, this will occur under specific conditions and after a long process of migrants' evaluation and categorisation.

From this perspective, a week after the above announcement, there has been proposed a new EU Blue Card Directive to replace the 2009 EU Blue Card Directive.[5] The proposal aims at addressing labour shortage, which is

[4] It is quite indicative that the 2015 percentage of female migrants internationally was 48.2% (United Nations 2015). Even though it is an important parameter, a detailed discussion of the gender dimension is beyond the scope of this book. For two interesting approaches, see Brah (1996); Kofman et al. (2000).

[5] According to the Council Directive 2009/50/EC of 25 May 2009, the EU Blue Card Directive defines the conditions of entry, residence and work of high-skilled non EU-citizens in any EU country, except the United Kingdom, Denmark and Ireland. Non-EU citizens can

expected to intensify within the next few years—especially, in certain sectors of the economy—due to criteria and demographic parameters (such as, the ageing of the EU population) already underlined, among others, by *Bertelsmann Stiftung*'s study. As it is clearly stated, "the proposal would entail faster, simpler and more inclusive access for highly skilled third-country nationals to the Member States' labour markets, better mobility within the EU and more rights for the beneficiaries" (European Parliament 2017: 6). Within a neoliberal context, the involvement of the private sector is deemed as absolutely necessary to meet the needs of the integration procedure (European Commission 2017b); besides, it is an indisputable fact that "there has been a considerable degree of privatization of migration control, and private actors and agencies play a more pronounced role in facilitating or detaining the flow of migrants" (Menz and Caviedes 2010: 8–9).

Hence, "the world has become more open to flows of goods and capital but more closed to the circulation of human bodies" (Mezzadra and Neilson 2013: 19). Nonetheless, those bodies deemed as capable of contributing to the accumulation of capital are allowed to move, according to the calculated needs of the labour market, in order to be integrated for *their own* "good" and "prosperity", while, at the same time, the whole process is taking place under the humanist pretext of "hospitality". It is within this frame that borders have proved to be "a regulator of labour markets" (Pellerin 2005: 56). For, "[t]he tendency to create the *world market* is directly given in the concept of capital itself. Every limit appears as a barrier to be overcome" (Marx 1973: 408; emphasis in the original). Depending on the demand for labour force and/or the socio-political balances within the Western world, borders are open or closed, whereas hotspots, detention centres and camps in European host countries, even in Turkey or Libya, are emptied or overcrowded. Thus, adopting Foucault's analytics on power (1991, 1998) and following the line of argument by Mezzadra and Neilson (2013), we suggest that we are witnessing both a negative and repressive function of borders as a means of migrants' brutal and inhumane exclusion, and a "productive" role as a significant part of the capitalist arsenal for the selection process and inclusion of the most appropriate labour force.

apply for a work permit that can be renewed. The target of the Directive is "to contribute to achieving these goals and addressing *labour shortages* by fostering the admission and mobility—for the purposes of highly qualified employment—of third-country nationals for stays of more than three months, in order to make the Community more attractive to such workers from around the world and sustain its *competitiveness* and *economic growth*" (European Union 2009: 17; emphasis added).

Accordingly, borders, as "sites of confrontation, contact, blocking, and passage" (Mezzadra and Neilson 2013: 27), perform another dual function as spaces of exclusion and, at the same time, spaces of resistance. For, it should be stressed that the temporary "opening" of the European borders was also the result of migrants' decisiveness and resolution to claim their entrance into the European territory. Therefore, it constituted a tactical retreat of European border politics—undoubtedly, through a series of new, even more "refined" criteria of exclusion, as, among others, the arbitrary dichotomy between "migrants" and "refugees"—towards the massive flow of migrants who, due to the relentless wars, the economic problems, the social unrest and the climate change in Africa and the Middle East, chose to fight for their entrance into the West at all costs. In other words, the European borders did, in fact, "open" temporarily also because their presence and function were collectively and decisively challenged by the subjects who attempted to "illegally" transcend them. Nonetheless, European countries, faced with these unprecedented and surplus migration flows, eventually strengthened their borders' symbolic status and literal presence, making them even more efficient and "productive" in this new era that the EU seems to inaugurate regarding migration control and management. And it is within the frame of exactly this rationale that we witnessed the closing of the European borders, to which we referred in the previous chapter. As a result, countries, like Turkey and Greece, are in a process of being transformed into extended Ellis Island, permanently or temporarily, in order to manage and control this "surplus population"; namely, to confine "the lever of capitalist accumulation, [...] a condition for the existence of the capitalist mode of production. [...] a disposable industrial reserve army, which belongs to capital just as absolutely as if the latter had bred it at its own cost" (Marx 1976: 784). Once again, the distinction between "migrants" and "refugees" and, consequently, between "illegal migrants" and "semi-legal" or "legal refugees" (i.e. asylum seekers) is at stake. At the same time, "[p]olicies that claim to exclude undocumented workers may often really be about allowing them in through side doors and back doors, so that they can be more readily exploited. [...]. In this context, migration control is really about regulating North-South relationships and maintaining inequality" (Castles 2004: 223).[6] From this perspective, it should not be

[6]A very characteristic example had been the Bracero Program, signed between the USA and Mexico in 1942, to deal with a severe labour shortage in the United States, especially in

regarded as accidental that the emergency support to several countries—among others, to Greece[7]—has proved to be a quite lucrative and profitable business, and a means for regaining social and political security, constituting, as we are going to see in the next chapter, a significant part of the whole "humanitarian industry".

And for all those who are still wondering why thousands of migrants did not end up safely to central and northern Europe, but were submitted to an endless torture for a "better life", when European countries did not open their borders, even to refugees "entitled" to be granted asylum, these people's deadly and painful journey gives us the answer. For, if someone fights in the cold waters of the Aegean Sea, having possibly lost in the sea or in another passage his/her loved ones; if s/he becomes the object of economic, sexual or any other kind of exploitation and abuse by traffickers, port authorities, policemen and border guards; if s/he has the painful experience of the twenty-first-century concentration camps or remains for days in a tent on the muddy ground of Idomeni camp or elsewhere; if s/he traverses half of Europe on foot; if s/he is regularly confronted with the derogatory gaze of a socially diffused racism; if s/he literally bleeds along the borders of Greece, Croatia or Hungary, then by arriving at the supposed "promised land", s/he will be ready to go over rather eagerly from the period of torture to the "humane" and "civilised" period of his/her discipline in the Western world. In other words, s/he will be ready to be constructed as a docile and productive body, as a body economically useful and politically subjected (Foucault 1991); namely, s/he will be ready to enter the sphere of bourgeois "legality" and "norms"—but, let us keep in mind that "what presents itself to us as bourgeois legality is nothing but the violence of the ruling class, a violence raised to an obligatory norm from the outset" (Luxemburg

agriculture. The Bracero Program, which lasted until December 1964, led to the generation of a flow of "illegal migrants". One of the main reasons was that many employers preferred to hire undocumented workers, since they were less cumbersome and not as expensive as "braceros" (Inda 2006).

[7] Greece had received over €1 billion between 2015 and the beginning of 2017, being "the biggest recipient of EU home affairs funding" (European Commission 2017c). And, on 27 July 2017, the European Commission announced a new wave of emergency support worth €209 million to help refugees in Greece. This includes the launch of the "Emergency Support To Integration & Accommodation" (ESTIA) programme, aiming at helping refugees and their families rent urban accommodation and providing them with cash assistance (European Commission 2017d).

1902: 3); hence, s/he will be ready to negotiate his/her labour force and, at last, his/her own existence in terms of destitution and under conditions literally unlivable. Eventually, those who will be "lucky" enough first to survive and then to enter central and northern Europe and staff its labour force are those who will have been chosen as the most appropriate and productive for capitalism, after an exhaustive procedure of evaluation and classification of their own subjectivity.[8] Besides, "[t]he existence of a class which possesses nothing but the ability to work is a necessary presupposition of capital" (Marx 2006: 30). After a long process of exposure to deadly dangers and humiliating conditions, migrants are actually condemned to a permanent state of exception that renders them the *par excellence* "bare lives" of twenty-first-century Western societies. At the same time, "the decisive fact is that, together with the process by which the exception everywhere becomes the rule, the realm of bare life – which is originally situated at the margins of the political order – gradually begins to coincide with the political realm, and exclusion and inclusion, outside and inside, *bios* and *zoē*, right and fact, enter into a zone of irreducible indistinction" (Agamben 1998: 9; emphasis in the original), bringing us to mind the surface of a Möbius strip, where there is, in fact, no inside and outside. Within this frame of the consolidation and diffusion of the exception, borders are becoming a mechanism constantly transformed, redesigned and diffused, through a complex nexus of technoscientific, military, political and humanitarian intervention and management of migration.

[8] For example, in autumn 2015, Norway and Denmark offered to male migrants language lessons, but also lessons of sexual behaviour, since, according to the dominant Western view, their cultural origins are rendering them *a priori* dangerous regarding their relationships with women. H.K. Rohde, a former head of the violent crime section of the Oslo Police Department, stated that "[t]here are lots of men who haven't learned that women have value [...] it is a cultural problem". Accordingly, Per Isdal, clinical psychologist, underlined that many refugees "come from cultures that are not gender equal and where women are the property of men. We have to help them *adapt* to their new culture" (cited in Higgins 2015; emphasis added). In December 2015, the Finnish government announced its decision to require asylum seekers to work for free and acknowledge a "national curriculum" on Finnish culture and society, attempting to launch a series of measures to tighten its migration policy. According to Prime Minister Juha Sipilä, these measures will not only "tighten our practices and erase possible attractiveness factors", but also boost migrants' self-esteem, since any kind of meaningful action, such as work, will help them relieve their frustration from idleness ... (*REUTERS* 2015).

References

Agamben, G. 1998. *Homo sacer. Sovereign Power and Bare Life*, tr. D. Heller-Roazen. Stanford, CA: Stanford University Press.

Agamben, G. 1999. *Remnants of Auschwitz. The Witness and the Archive*, tr. D. Heller-Roazen. New York: Zone Books.

Arendt, H. 1994. "We Refugees". In M. Robinson (ed.), *Altogether Elsewhere. Writers on Exile.* Boston/London: Faber and Faber.

BASF. 2015. "Online Report 2015. Vocational Training and Career Development". https://report.basf.com/2015/en/managements-report/working-at-basf/training.html (Accessed 14 October 2017).

Bertelsmann Stiftung. 2015. "Study: The Labor Market Will Need More Immigration from Non-EU Countries in the Future", 27 March. https://www.bertelsmann-stiftung.de/en/topics/aktuelle-meldungen/2015/maerz/immigration-from-non-eu-countries/ (Accessed 14 January 2016).

Brah, A. 1996. *Cartographies of Diaspora. Contesting Identities.* London/New York: Routledge.

Brown, W. 2010. *Walled States. Waning Sovereignty.* New York: Zone Books.

Castles, S. 2004. "Why Migration Policies Fail". *Ethnic and Racial Studies*, 27(2): 205–227. https://doi.org/10.1080/0141987042000177306.

Connolly, K. 2015. "Germany Greets Refugees with Help and Kindness at Munich Central Station". *The Guardian*, 3 September. http://www.theguardian.com/world/2015/sep/03/germany-refugees-munich-central-station (Accessed 5 September 2015).

De Martino, C. 2015. "European Commission Called for a Better Use of EU Funds in Order to Support Refugees' Crisis". *EU-LOGOS*, 10 October. https://europe-liberte-securite-justice.org/2015/10/10/european-commission-called-for-a-better-use-of-eu-funds-in-order-to-support-refugees-crisis/ (Accessed 16 September 2015).

Derrida, J. and Dufourmantelle, A. 2000. *Of Hospitality*, tr. R. Bowlby. Stanford, CA: Stanford University Press.

European Commission. 2016. "A First Evaluation Based on the 2014 EU Labour Force Survey ad hoc Module. How are Refugees Faring on the Labour Market in Europe?". https://ec.europa.eu/migrant-integration/librarydoc/how-are-refugees-faring-on-the-labour-market-in-europe (Accessed 16 October 2017).

European Commission. 2017a. "Press Statement by Commissioners Avramopoulos and Thyssen on the Launch of the EU Skills Profile Tool for Non-EU Citizens", 20 June. http://europa.eu/rapid/press-release_SPEECH-17-1727_en.htm (Accessed 16 October 2017).

European Commission. 2017b. "Ensuring Effective Legal Pathways to Europe". https://ec.europa.eu/home-affairs/sites/homeaffairs/files/what-we-do/

policies/european-agenda-migration/20170927_factsheet_ensuring_effective_legal_pathways_to_europe_en.pdf (Accessed 15 October 2017).

European Commission. 2017c. "Statement by Commissioner Avramopoulos during His Visit to Lesvos, Greece", 18 January. http://europa.eu/rapid/press-release_SPEECH-17-87_en.pdf (Accessed 16 October 2017).

European Commission. 2017d. "Press Release: EU Launches New Humanitarian Programme for the Integration & Accommodation of Refugees in Greece", 27 July. http://europa.eu/rapid/press-release_IP-17-2121_en.htm (Accessed 15 October 2017).

European Parliament. 2016. "Labour Market Integration of Refugees: Strategies and Good Practices". http://www.europarl.europa.eu/RegData/etudes/STUD/2016/578956/IPOL_STU(2016)578956_EN.pdf (Accessed 15 October 2017).

European Parliament. 2017. "Revision of the Blue Card Directive". http://www.europarl.europa.eu/RegData/etudes/BRIE/2017/603942/EPRS_BRI%282017%29603942_EN.pdf (Accessed 16 October 2017).

European Union. 2009. "Council Directive 2009/50/EC of 25 May 2009 on the Conditions of Entry and Residence of Third-country Nationals for the Purposes of Highly Qualified Employment". *Official Journal of the European Union*, 18 June. http://eur-lex.europa.eu/legal-content/EN/TXT/PDF/?uri=CELEX:32009L0050&from=EN (Accessed 9 November 2017).

Foucault, M. 1991. *Discipline and Punish. The Birth of the Prison*, tr. A. Sheridan. London/New York: Penguin Books.

Foucault, M. 1998. *The History of Sexuality. Volume 1. The Will to Knowledge*, tr. R. Hurley. London/New York: Penguin Books.

Foucault, M. 2003. *"Society Must Be Defended". Lectures at the Collège de France, 1975-76*, tr. D. Macey. New York: Picador.

Fratzscher, M. and Junker, S. 2015. "Integrating Refugees: A Long-term, Worthwhile Investment". *DIW Economic Bulletin*, 45/46: 612–616. https://www.diw.de/documents/publikationen/73/diw_01.c.519306.de/diw_econ_bull_2015-45-4.pdf (Accessed 9 November 2017).

Fuchs, J., Kubis, A., and Schneider, L. 2015. "Zuwanderungsbedarf aus Drittstaaten in Deutschland bis 2050". Gütersloh: Bertelsmann Stiftung. https://www.bertelsmann-stiftung.de/fileadmin/files/BSt/Publikationen/GrauePublikationen/Studie_IB_Zuwanderungsbedarf_aus_Drittstaaten_in_Deutschland_bis_2050_2015.pdf (Accessed 14 May 2016).

Hengst, B. and Sperber, S. 2015. "Flüchtlinge am Münchner Hauptbahnhof Start in ein neues Leben". *Spiegel Online*, 6 September. http://www.spiegel.de/politik/deutschland/fluechtlinge-am-hauptbahnhof-muenchen-erschoepfung-und-zuversicht-a-1051656.html (Accessed 9 November 2017).

Higgins, A. 2015. "Norway Offers Migrants a Lesson in How to Treat Women". *The New York Times*, 19 December. http://www.nytimes.com/2015/12/20/

world/europe/norway-offers-migrants-a-lesson-in-how-to-treat-women.html (Accessed 3 February 2016).

Inda, J.X. 2006. *Targeting Immigrants. Government, Technology, and Ethics.* Malden, MA: Blackwell Publishing.

Kofman, E., Phizacklea, A., Raghuram, P., and Sales, R. 2000. *Gender and International Migration in Europe. Employment, Welfare and Politics.* London/New York: Routledge.

Levi, P. 2015. *If this is a man.* In *The Complete Works of Primo Levi*, vol. 1, tr. S. Woolf. New York: Liveright Publishing Corporation.

Luxemburg, R. 1902. "Réponse au camarade E. Vandervelde". *Neue Zeit.* https://www.marxists.org/francais/luxembur/works/1902/rl19020514.htm (Accessed 14 October 2017).

Marx, K. 1973. *Grundrisse. Foundations of the Critique of Political Economy*, tr. M. Nicolaus. New York: Vintage Books.

Marx, K. 1976. *Capital. Vol. I*, tr. B. Fowkes. London/New York: Penguin Books.

Marx, K. 2006. *Wage Labour and Capital. Value, Price and Profit.* New York: International Publishers.

Menz, G. and Caviedes, A. 2010. "Introduction: Patterns, Trends, and (Ir) Regularities in the Politics and Economics of Labour Migration in Europe". In G. Menz and A. Caviedes (eds.), *Labour Migration in Europe.* Basingstoke, UK: Palgrave Macmillan.

Mezzadra, S. and Neilson, B. 2013. *Border as Method, or, the Multiplication of Labour.* Durham/London: Duke University Press.

Ong, A. 2006. *Neoliberalism as Exception. Mutations in Citizenship and Sovereignty.* Durham/London: Duke University Press.

Pellerin, H. 2005. "Borders, Migration and Economic Integration: Towards a New Political Economy of Borders". In E. Zureik and M.B. Salter (eds.), *Global Surveillance and Policing. Borders, Security, Identity.* Cullompton: Willan Publishing.

REUTERS. 2015. "Finland Says Asylum Seekers Should Work for Free", 8 December. http://www.reuters.com/article/us-europe-migrants-finland/finland-says-asylum-seekers-should-work-for-free-idUSKBN0TR2MK20151208 (Accessed 27 October 2017).

RTBF. 2015. "Faut-il voir les réfugiés comme une chance en termes sociaux et économiques?", 15 September. http://www.rtbf.be/info/dossier/les-refugies-et-moi-les-reponses-a-vos-questions/detail_accueillir-les-refugies-accroit-les-pesrpectives-de-croissance-de-l-europe?id=9080700 (Accessed 3 February 2016).

Schmieding, H. 2015. "Migration: Notes on the Potential Impact on Europe". http://blog.berenberg.de/migration-notes-on-the-potential-impact-on-europe/ (Accessed 9 January 2017).

Siemens AG. 2015. "Press Release: Siemens Introduces Sustainable Program for Integrating Refugees", 29 September. https://www.siemens.com/press/en/pressrelease/index.php?content%5B%5D=Corp&search=refugees&date-1-dd=14&date-1-mm=10&date-1=2014&date-2-dd=14&date-2-mm=10&date-2=2016&intern=1 (Accessed 14 October 2017).

Süddeutsche Zeitung. 2015. "Airbus-Chef Enders fordert Öffnung des Arbeitsmarkts", 26 October. http://www.sueddeutsche.de/wirtschaft/fluechtlingskrise-in-deutschland-airbus-chef-enders-fordert-oeffnung-des-arbeitsmarkts-1.2708339 (Accessed 26 October 2015).

UNHCR. 2015. "Interim Survey Results on the Profile of Persons from Syria Arriving at the Greek Borders". http://www.ilsole24ore.com/pdf2010/Editrice/ILSOLE24ORE/ILSOLE24ORE/Online/_Oggetti_Correlati/Documenti/Notizie/2015/09/scanning-migranti-grecia.pdf (Accessed 19 January 2016).

United Nations. 2015. "Trends in International Migration Stock: The 2015 Revision". http://www.un.org/en/development/desa/population/migration/data/estimates2/data/UN_MigrantStockTotal_2015.xlsx (Accessed 28 November 2017).

Zimmermann, N. 2015. "Germany's Challenge: Integration of Refugees". *Deutsche Welle*, 8 September. http://www.dw.com/en/germanys-challenge-integration-of-refugees/a-18702361 (Accessed 18 January 2016).

CHAPTER 4

Borders' Diffusion as a Response to the "Humanist Crisis": Towards a Military-Humanitarian Nexus

Abstract This chapter focuses on the current rhetoric regarding borders and the European migration policy that are built on two complementary foundations. On the one hand, migrants are represented as a multiform "threat" that violently invades the European territory and, on the other hand, as a helpless "victim" revealing a deep "humanist crisis". Our purpose is to study this humanitarian-military nexus of European migration politics that is based upon "states of emergency", such as in Lampedusa and Idomeni, leading to borders' constant transformation and diffusion.

Keywords Borders • Humanist crisis • Humanitarian aid • Militarisation • EUROSUR

As migrants are subjected to endless sufferings and transformed into the *par excellence* object of exploitation, depending on the capitalist needs, a series of new control mechanisms and new types of borders is being invented, expanded and diffused throughout the body politic; nowadays, borders are "constitutive of political life. [...], borders are not natural, neutral nor static but historically contingent, politically charged, dynamic phenomena that first and foremost involve people and their everyday lives" (Vaughan-Williams 2009: 1). The dominant rhetoric about borders and, consequently, EU migration politics are built upon two complementary foundations. On the one hand, migrants are represented as a multiform

T. Lagios et al., *Borders, Bodies and Narratives of Crisis in Europe*,
https://doi.org/10.1007/978-3-319-75586-1_4

"threat" violently invading the European territory; on the other hand, they are represented as helpless and voiceless "victims". In other words, sometimes migrants are represented as "illegal" migrants, as we have already stressed in the previous chapters, and other times as "refugees" in desperate need of our protection and humanitarian aid. However, both views are, in fact, the two sides of the same coin, constructing the migrant's identity as a subject who has lost its *human* qualities and, for this reason, must passively accept the future offered by the Western philanthropy and humanist politics. Irrespective of the particular identity attributed to migrants—"threat" or "victim"—there is systematically constructed a complex grid of military and political management of migration, on the one hand, and humanitarian (usually, represented as "non-political") intervention, on the other hand.

To begin with, the dominant narrative on the migrant as a "threat" is strongly legitimised, as we are going to see in the next chapter, through the medical discourse and, equally, through the construction of the migrant's identity as a "criminal". As we have already highlighted in Chap. 2, this identity is reproduced in newspaper articles, scientific studies and school books that, among others, correlate migration with an increase in crime, as well as in EU official statements that liken, as we are going to see, transnational border entities, such as EUROSUR, to a levee against "slave trade"[1] and drug trafficking.[2] And, on the occasion of the ISIS attacks across Europe, there is emerging a specific rhetoric that, instead of dealing with terrorism and its causes, is oftentimes based on the *a priori* criminalisation and psychopathologisation of both the Islamic culture and the migrant identity itself. A characteristic example is the following statement by the Greek Defence Minister Panos Kammenos at *The Times*, in April 2015: "Europe has to realise that by keeping Greece stable, the West's front against ISIS is secure. But if pushed out or forced out of the Eurozone … waves of undocumented migrants, including radical elements, will spill in from Turkey, making their way to the heart of the West" (cited in Carassava and Aldrick 2015).

[1] However, in contrast to the dominant portraiture about "slave traders", systematically constructed by politicians and the media, the reality is far different. As Khosravi emphatically underlines through his personal experience, "[h]uman smuggling is recurrently misrepresented by the media and politicians as an entirely 'mafia'-controlled criminality, but this is not the case" (2010: 21).

[2] Characteristically, see European Commission (2011); European Commission (2013).

If we now turn our attention to the other side of the coin, which places the migrant in the position of the "passive victim" in need of humanitarian aid and protection, we face a *prima facie* paradox in contradistinction to the abovementioned rhetoric. Our starting point will be the tragedy of Lampedusa. On 3 October 2013, a small boat, having departed from the shores of Libya and being filled to the brim with migrants, is shipwrecked near Lampedusa, in Sicily, failing to reach the European territory. Within the next few days, the death toll rises to tragic proportions, with the number of migrants who are recovered dead from the sea reaching 368 (Sunderland 2014). Despite the fact that, according to official statistics, from 1988 until 2014 thousands of migrants lost their lives on Europe's southern borders alone,[3] this event immediately became the symbol of the "refugee drama", condensing all the sorrow and "mourning" of the Western world towards the "humanist crisis". Pope Francis posted on Twitter, calling all the faithful to pray for the victims,[4] whereas the Italian Prime Minister Enrico Letta called for an emergency cabinet meeting, declaring the day following the tragic shipwreck as a day of "national mourning". Within this context, José Manuel Barroso, president of the European Committee, visited Lampedusa to pay respects to the victims and express his solidarity with its residents. Meanwhile, TV crews and reporters arrived at the small port for live broadcasts, rendering this tragedy a media spectacle, whereas, until very recently, similar shipwrecks went unnoticed. Now, these "sorrow fiestas" in a totally tragic scenery were a show of an unprecedented sensitivity and humanism towards "refugees" who were attempting, against all odds and by any means necessary, to enter the "promised land" and, for this reason, were represented as "embodied eternal human suffering" (Khosravi 2010: 73).

[3] According to International Centre for Migration Policy Development (ICMPD), at least 10,000 died in the Mediterranean in their attempt to cross the European borders in the decade 1993–2003. Accordingly, UNITED for Intercultural Action, an international NGO, estimates that the total number of people who lost their lives during their attempt to cross Europe's southern borders is about 14,600 for the period 1993–November 2012, while, according to Fortress Europe, that number rises to 14,757 deaths for the period 1988–end of June 2014. More generally, International Organization of Migration (IOM) estimates that between January and September 2014, at least 4,077 migrants died in their attempt to reach various destinations around the world, whereas since 2000, it is estimated that at least 40,000 migrants have died. To these numbers, there are not included those who are still missing and may never be found (Grant 2011; Last and Spijkerboer 2014).

[4] He wrote: "Lord, have mercy! Too often we are blinded by our comfortable lives, and refuse to see those dying at our doorstep" (Pope Francis 2013).

Consequently, there was attributed to the, until recently, "illegal migrants" a more socially acceptable and viable identity—that of the "beleaguered, impoverished refugee"—and a better sounding voice to narrate their experiences, which, of course, should fit in the dominant narrative constructed by the Western collective imaginary. An "industry of mourning" was spectacularly established through the constant videotaping and circulation of photos of the dead bodies that the sea kept washing up for days, through the lachrymose speeches by politicians and other officials, as well as through the representation of the, until then, "illegal migrants" as sad, tortured and likeable fellow human beings. Nonetheless, beneath and beyond the limelight, this mourning did not actually concern the actual persons involved and their own stories and experiences, but some anonymous bodies; bodies that provoke, at the same time, either sympathy ("refugees") or fear ("migrants"), constructing this dual identity of the "Other" and reminding us of the dual reality of medieval madmen, "a spectacle well known to the observer from outside; not a figure of the *cosmos*, but merely of the order of the *aevum*" (Foucault 2006: 25; emphasis in the original).

Within this "state of emergency" that is constitutive of contemporary power relations, where critique and opposition are, in fact, unacceptable (Mattei 2010), we became witnesses of the contradictory attempt to devaluate migrants' lives through the imposition upon them of the status of the victim.[5] For, this mechanism of victimisation is, indeed, the epitome and "essence of the humanitarian industry" (Filippidis 2013). From this perspective, by attempting to "critically evaluate and oppose the conditions under which certain human lives are more vulnerable than others, and thus certain human lives are more grievable than others" (Butler 2004: 30), we claim that this "state of emergency", this "humanist crisis", has been used as a point of departure not only for the aforementioned humanitarian culture,[6] but, equally, for a series of significant transformations in the technologies of migration control and European border politics, in general.

[5] However, as it becomes manifest through migrants' personal stories and daily struggles, the status of the victim does not imply an irrevocable passivity and the absence of any kind of agency; "[a] victim image opens up possibilities not only for partaking in lucrative emergency aid projects but also for the creation of compassionate bonds with important social actors [...]" (Utas 2005: 409).

[6] Historically, the whole culture of humanitarianism has been built upon the notions of "crisis" and "emergency". For some interesting examples, see Pandolfi (2003, 2010).

It is within this humanitarian-military complex that, on 9 October 2013, the European Parliament voted in favour of the relevant regulation[7] and on 22 October 2013 brought into effect the European Border Surveillance System (EUROSUR), which officially began its operations on 2 December 2013. According to its guidelines, EUROSUR "establishes a common framework for the exchange of information and for the cooperation between Member States and the Agency in order to improve situational awareness and to increase reaction capability at the external borders of the Member States of the Union ('external borders') for the purpose of detecting, preventing and combating illegal immigration and cross-border crime and contributing to ensuring the protection and saving the lives of migrants ('EUROSUR')" (European Union 2013: 14). Even from the first lines of the operating guidelines, it becomes evident to the observant reader that the crucial issue at stake is the articulation of the intensification of the military control for the population's security under the, rather vague, humanitarian pretext of rescuing migrants' lives. As the Dutch Member of the European Parliament and proponent of EUROSUR Jan Mulder emphasised, "[o]nly by having a pan-European border surveillance system we can prevent the Mediterranean from becoming a graveyard for refugees trying to cross it in unseaworthy small boats in search of a better life in Europe. To prevent a tragedy like that off Lampedusa from happening again, rapid intervention is necessary" (European Parliament 2013a). Accordingly, the German Member of the European Parliament, currently heading the European People's Party Group, Manfred Weber underlined that "EUROSUR is a contribution to improve the cooperation of the EU member states in frontier-defence affairs, but also to prevent refugee dramas" (European Parliament 2013b); namely, first defence and then prevention. On the same wavelength, the press release on 29 November 2013, characteristically entitled "EUROSUR kicks off: new tools to save migrants' lives and prevent crime at EU borders" (European Commission 2013), emphatically reveals how there is gradually constructed an unbreakable bond between security for the body politic *inside* borders and demand for humanitarian aid for migrants *outside* borders.

Undeniably, this systematic attempt to intensify and, in essence, militarise border control is welcomed and reinforced not only by politicians, but

[7] EUROSUR was approved by 479 votes to 101, with 20 abstentions (European Parliament 2013a).

almost by all those who participate, in one way or another, in migration management, leading eventually to the concealment of the demand for security under the juxtaposition of "flows of humanitarian aid" vis-à-vis "migration flows". For Stefano Di Carlo, Médecins Sans Frontières (MSF) Italy Head of Mission, "[a]s long as *the desperate are forced* to take this perilous route, Italy and the EU must stand up and respond to the *humanitarian disaster* unfolding on their doorstep. Thousands of lives would be at stake should international waters, where many tragic shipwrecks occur, fail to be *actively patrolled*" (Médecins Sans Frontières 2014; emphasis added). This technoscientific, militarised mechanism of the Western world for population control, surveillance and management has "recruited" a multitude of persons and institutions, with different starting points and, occasionally, quite different goals; from various NGOs and the Red Cross to the Hellenic Centre for Disease Control & Prevention (HCDCP) at the centre of many Greek cities, up to the Corpo Italiano di Soccorso dell' Ordine di Malta (CISOM).

Unfortunately, the tragedy of Lampedusa has not been either the first or the last time that a "state of (humanitarian) emergency" was constructed in a spectacular fashion, demanding radical solutions and leading to the militarisation of control, and vice versa, without preventing, in the least, the loss of migrants' lives.[8] Within the context of borders' closing, at the beginning of 2016, there was erected a makeshift migrant camp next to the Greece-FYR of Macedonia border, near the village of Idomeni. The camp's inhumane conditions were daily reproduced in the Greek and European media, whereas the terms "humanist crisis" and "state of emergency" were unceasingly repeated in the public discourse.[9] EU officials, politicians, NGOs visited regularly the camp, giving lachrymose speeches. At the beginning of March 2016, ERT, the state-owned public radio and television broadcaster for Greece, adjusted its entire programme around this very subject, culminating in the live broadcast of the news from the Idomeni camp, on 7 March 2016,[10] to be followed by the introduction of

[8] Just a few months after the tragedy of Lampedusa, 11 Afghani people, including eight children, lost their lives, when their boat sank near the small Greek island of Farmakonisi, in the Aegean Sea, on 20 January 2014. People who survived claimed that they were towed at great speed by the Greek coastguard back towards Turkey (Amnesty International 2015).

[9] Quite characteristically, Apostolos Tzitzikostas, governor of the Greek region of Central Macedonia, stated at *The Guardian*: "It's a huge *humanitarian crisis*. I have [asked] the government to declare *a state of emergency* in the area" (cited in Smith 2016; emphasis added).

[10] See, http://webtv.ert.gr/ert1/eidiseis/07mar2016-2100-deltio-idiseon/.

short news in Arabic exclusively for refugees on a daily basis, on 24 March.[11] And, on 15 March 2016, Dimitris Avramopoulos, EU Commissioner for Migration, Home Affairs and Citizenship, and Ioannis Mouzalas, the Greek Minister of Migration Policy, visited Idomeni. Avramopoulos stated: "What we see today in Idomeni should be the last chapter of a tragedy that must not be repeated. We need to stop it. [...], we have to stop migrant smugglers from undermining the legitimacy and implementation of our common rules, and from limitlessly exploiting vulnerable people" (European Commission 2016a).

Within this frame, EU and Turkey agreed in Brussels on a series of actions, on 18 March 2016; more specifically, "to end the irregular migration from Turkey to the EU by breaking the business model of the smugglers and offering migrants an alternative to putting their lives at risk", as well as "to restore a legal and orderly admission system for those entitled to international protection in line with EU and international law" (European Commission 2016b). For this purpose, Turkey had to take immediately any measures necessary to prevent the formation of new sea or land routes for "illegal" migration. In return, EU would speed up the disbursement of the initially allocated €3 billion to address the immediate needs of refugees in Turkey, whereas emergency support would be provided to Greece, as well (Council of Europe 2016). Only a week after the relevant paperwork had been signed, on 24 March 2016, on the very same day that the news in Arabic was introduced into the Greek public television, the violent evacuation of the Idomeni camp took place, with the participation of hundreds police officers. Migrants were transferred, "for their own good", to organised "reception centres" in the region near Thessaloniki; very quickly, most of them proved to be nothing more than miserable prisons. So, we became witnesses of another police operation that was covered under the guise of "humanitarian intervention" and presented as a "rational" solution to the "humanist crisis", with migrants being once again imprisoned in detention centres under literally unlivable conditions. In other words, we became witnesses "both of the humanitarianization of international crisis management and of the politicization of the nongovernmental humanitarian field", of this "merging of politics and humanitarianism" (Fassin 2007: 510), that lies at the heart of contemporary biopolitical societies.

[11] See, http://webtv.ert.gr/category/ert1/eidiseis/news-prosfyges/. To this direction, the Greek Prime Minister, Alexis Tsipras, commented on Twitter: "We are greeting the initiative by ERT and ANA-MPA [Athens News Agency – Macedonian Press Agency] to broadcast valid information for refugees in their language" (2016).

Equally indicative of the detrimental consequences of this "merging of politics and humanitarianism" are the conditions in the five Greek hotspots in the Aegean Sea. The joint statement of over 100 solidarity and activist groups, published in October 2017, is quite revealing: "[s]ix people who were seeking refuge and protection in Europe died in Moria last winter, their deaths linked to inhumane winter living conditions. [...]. Approximately 5000 people currently live in Moria camp, which has a capacity of around 2000. This includes the seriously ill, the disabled, pregnant women, many children including unaccompanied minors, and survivors of torture and other trauma" (Open The Islands 2017). Accordingly, Refugee Support Aegean (RSA), a non-profit organisation, underlines the severe living conditions and the acute problems in the Greek hotspots. For example, the hotspot in Vathy (Samos) has a capacity of 700 persons, but hosts more than 2,400 persons, whereas hotspot VIAL (Chios), which is located in an abandoned aluminium factory, has a capacity of around 894 persons, but currently hosts almost 2,000 persons (RSA 2017). Equally, EU official reports underline the same inhumane conditions at Moria, as well as in other hotspots and detention centres: "the conditions of detention deteriorated rapidly as the Centres [Moria and VIAL on Lesvos and Chios, respectively] became overcrowded and had to accommodate people for weeks on end rather than a few days as intended. There were problems with the quality of drinking water, food, basic health care provision and addressing the needs of vulnerable groups. The conditions in the closed Section B of Moria Centre were particularly poor and could be considered as inhuman and degrading. [...]. A number of credible allegations of physical ill-treatment of foreign national detainees by police officers were received at Thessaloniki and Petrou Ralli Special holding facilities. Rigorous action should be taken to counter acts of ill-treatment" (Council of Europe 2017: 5–6). Nonetheless, in February 2017, I. Mouzalas, Minister of Migration Policy, responded to criticism, following the death of three people at Moria, by expressing his hope that these deaths "will make us all wiser" (*ERT International* 2017). At the time these lines are being written [December 2017], the horrible conditions are still present.[12] And, even though they are incessantly being reported by migrants, activists, interna-

[12] For a recent article on the conditions on the island of Samos, published at *The Guardian* in November 2017, see Christides and Stefatou (2017). More generally, on migrants' ill-treatment in Greece, see also Sitaropoulos (2017).

tional organisations, even by the EU, which, despite its official policies, keeps warning Greece about the possible penalties for migrants' ill-treatment, most migrants remain invisible and trapped within these facilities, within this painful nexus of humanitarian and military management, within this "state of emergency" that few people dare to question.

Nonetheless, migrants do sometimes invade the public sphere, making "material and psychosocial spaces porous [...] where public and private intermingle, deviance and norm are renegotiated, zones of exploitation and justice are rearranged, formal and informal situations are reassembled" (Papadopoulos and Tsianos 2007: 226). Several personal stories emerge within this context, amidst borders, camps and dangerous routes to Europe. But, despite their *real* suffering and their *personal* stories, migrants are usually represented more as characters in a dystopian film and less as human beings with rights, desires and dreams: "the protagonists of the catastrophes of this world are subjected to a biographical denuding that turns them into anonymous and a-historical figures, merely populating destroyed landscapes and standardised infrastructures of mass nutrition and relief" (Filippidis 2013). Within this frame, migrants have only painful ways to become visible again; through their hunger strikes, their riots, their struggles.

Despite their decisiveness and impetuosity, these struggles usually hit against the *Walls* of Europe that are constantly being challenged and, for this reason, re-designed and re-built. From this perspective, another significant point, linked to the intensification of the technoscientific mechanisms of control, as well as to the transformation of borders *per se*, is the deep crisis of the so-called European Integration; at least, in comparison with the dominant rhetoric and its connotations before the "crisis". Quite indicative of this new historical condition is, among others, the recent referendum in Great Britain and the result in favour of "Brexit"; a historical condition that is gradually leading to a new page in the history of the idea of Europe as an *Imagined Community*, to borrow Benedict Anderson's term (2006). In the era of migration management and migrants' "rational" distribution across the European territory, we are witnessing a restructuring and re-building of the "Schengen Area" on both a political and an economic level. This procedure turns out to be of paramount importance, since Schengen is considered by the EU as "one of the major achievements of European integration" (European Commission 2016c:

2).[13] From this perspective, there appeared in the forefront a series of statements by European officials, who envision and work hard for the transition into a different kind of "European Integration", where, primarily, the flow of capital will remain unhindered; besides, as it has been underlined by the European Commission in its proposed Roadmap for restoring Schengen in March 2016, "[t]he free exchange of goods within the EU currently accounts for more than €2,800 billion in value and 1,700 million tonnes in volume" (ibid: 3). Quite characteristically, Fabrice Leggeri, chief executive officer at Frontex, underlined that "[m]ember states must understand that in place of deploying hundreds of police at their national borders, it would be more useful to send them to the (EU's) external border". And, he continued: "The real frontier is Lampedusa, Lesbos and Melilla. [...]. We have to go towards a more integrated management of our borders [...] which would allow Frontex in certain cases to intervene in a crisis without waiting for the member states in question to ask for it" (*SigmaLive* 2015). In the same spirit, European Council president, Donald Tusk, stated emphatically that "[s]aving Schengen is a race against time and we are determined to win that race. Without effective control on our external borders, the Schengen rules will not survive" (cited in Holehouse, Fraser 2015). Thus, even though "we have come to hear much about the project of a *Europe without frontiers*", European borders "endure, incorporated and cited now in European discourses of integration" (Sidaway 2007: 175; emphasis in the original). Thus, Europe's and, consequently, the Western world's external borders are acquiring a different significance. As a result, given that "[s]pace is not simply a matter of inside and outside but composed of multiple strata" (Walters 2006: 154), it should be stressed that nowadays the right and the chance to experience and live in the "People's Europe" tends to be exclusively for Europeans.

Taking the above into consideration, we are now in a position to better understand and evaluate both European migration politics and borders' transformations. During the last years, we are facing a technoscientific transition from the barbed wire and the border guard to satellite images, non-human aircrafts and drones. Through this transition, the static, to an extent, status of the barbed wire is complemented by the flexibility and ubiquity of drones and thermal cameras. At the same time, the communi-

[13] Within this context, the "Updated Schengen Rules" were published in September 2017 (European Commission 2017).

cation among scattered border guards is facilitated and enriched by databases and satellites that represent "migration flows" by thousand pixels on the screens at EUROSUR central operations hub in Warsaw. Faced with the complexity of this new control mechanism, the border guard has become, to an extent, insufficient and obsolete as the subject of control and surveillance, being also complemented and supported by private, particularly profitable security companies, health services, NGOs, and so on. Obviously, these shifts did not take place overnight. Even from the mid-1990s, this mechanism has already been under construction, with the introduction of the information systems Schengen Information System (SIS), Supplément d' Information Requis à l' Entrée Nationale (SIRENE), EURODAC and Visa Information System (VIS) for the enactment of the treaties of Schengen (1985), Amsterdam (1999) and Dublin (1997, 2003, 2013), as well as the founding of FRONTEX (2004).[14] In 2007, the British Home Office emphasised that "[b]order control can no longer just be a fixed line on a map. Using new technology, particularly biometrics, and new approaches to managing risk and intelligence, we must create a new offshore line of defence, [...]. A strong border is good for travellers, good for industry, national security and the economy" (Home Office 2007: 2). Thus, this process of digitisation and militarisation of migrants' control and surveillance, as well as of large population groups, is nowadays without precedent.

As we stressed in the previous chapter, borders have a dual function, aiming not only at controlling, recording and managing migration flows, but also at creating mechanisms of illegalisation and devaluation of particular population groups. In this way, migrants, as we have seen, are sometimes represented as a "threat" and other times as voiceless "victims" deserving Western philanthropy. Under this prism, their arrest is interpreted as "rescue", their labour under humiliating conditions as "integration" and their imprisonment in concentration camps, detention centres and hotspots as "humanitarian aid". In this way, humanitarian intervention does not simply function as a pretext for borders' militarisation and migration control but, equally, as a constitutive element of this procedure. It is this merging of humanitarian and military intervention that conceals the surveillance and disciplinary mechanisms under the guise of philanthropy and humanism, rendering these mechanisms even more diffused, more penetrative, more effective. This articulation has been equally con-

[14] On SIS, SIRENE, EURODAC and VIS, see Broeders (2007, 2011); Mathiesen (1999).

firmed and legitimised by the ease that all these detention centres and hotspots—introduced as humanitarian—were transformed into closed detention centres, according to the specific demands and criteria of European migration policy. Besides, within this Panopticon,[15] within this all-encompassing "dataveillance",[16] "it is precisely the most subordinate and marginalized groups who will find their identities most difficult to authenticate. From downtown banking halls to city airport terminals, the techniques of dataveillance will continually inscribe and reinscribe a manufactured border between the licit and illicit worlds" (Amoore and De Goede 2005: 168). In other words, borders are functioning as a "threshold between the inside and the outside" (Vaughan-Williams 2009: 74), as dividing lines between those subjects, whose human essence and the—supposedly universal and recognised through a series of declarations—human rights are largely deemed as given, and those non-subjects, for whom nothing is given and upon whom a permanent "state of exception" is being imposed; of course, it is an exception that will always be the cause for emotional declarations—as it had been the case with the death of Alan Kurdi, in September 2015[17]—and simultaneously the fuse for a state of even more exceptions.

[15] By combining the term "Ban" by Jean-Luc Nancy, as it was reformulated by Giorgio Agamben, and the "Panopticon" by Michel Foucault, Didier Bigo introduced the concept of "Ban-opticon" to describe the situation in Western societies, as it has been consolidated after 9/11. For Bigo, the "Ban-opticon" is characterised "by the exceptionalism of power (rules of emergency and their tendency to become permanent), by the way it excludes certain groups in the name of their future potential behaviour (profiling) and by the way it normalizes the non-excluded through its production of normative imperatives, the most important of which is free movement (the so-called four freedoms of circulation of the EU: concerning goods, capital, information, services and persons)" (2008: 32). Accordingly, Bigo claims that the detention camp for migrants is within the frame of the Banopticon the equivalent of what the prison is within the frame of the Foucauldian Panopticon (2007).

[16] According to Clarke's definition, "*[d]ataveillance* is the systematic use of personal data systems in the investigation or monitoring of the actions or communications of one or more persons" (1988: 499; emphasis in the original). On the concept of "dataveillance", see Clarke (1988); Levi and Wall (2004); Amoore and De Goede (2005).

[17] Quite indicative of the exploitation of these tragedies is that even in the case of Alan Kurdi, for whom so many tears were spilt, so many declarations were made, so many pieces of art were created, the boy's name remained wrongly known as "Aylan", as it had been initially transmitted, and no one felt the need to correct this mistake. As Butler is wondering: "Will we feel compelled to learn how to say these names and to remember them?" (2004: 37).

Nonetheless, this condition is not just an upgrade at the level of technological means and border effectiveness, but also a widening of the concept of the border *per se*. Besides, as it has been already made clear, the act of delimitation itself constitutes primarily a social and political practice. Therefore, the border does not constitute a univocal concept, but tends nowadays to be everywhere as "it is both portable (the plastic card) and virtual (the database)" (Lyon 2005: 66). From this perspective, beyond the usual criticism with regards to the "proper" or "erroneous" use of scientific knowledge and technological means, it is necessary to highlight the multifaceted implications of these processes, since limitations and exclusions tend to extend to increasingly wider population groups, deemed as "deviant" from the established societal norms or actively resisting them. Therefore, borders aim not only at separating the "civilised" and "developed" West from the "barbaric" and "uncivilised" East, the "centre" from the "periphery", and excluding hermetically anyone not born in its territory, but also at being deadly for those deemed as surplus and porous for those potentially exploitable. In this context, migration operates also as a test tube for new practices for the control, regulation and discipline of the social body; namely, as a model for the management of any form of diversity and every "Other" *inside* and *outside* borders.[18] Through this transition from "Fortress Europe" to Europe as a "gated community",[19] through the constant diffusion of borders, through the incessant redefinition of who is constituting the "inside" and who is constituting the necessary "outside" of Western societies, the state of exception tends to become the rule of the body politic; a rule with an extremely unstable character and a continuously expanding target. For, the focal point of the above practices is, indeed, an element that has been in the forefront since the late eighteenth century: the human body.

[18] As it is rightly asserted, "'[i]nside' and 'outside' are not clearly demarcated; the inside relies on the outside for its coherence and for the cognition of its limits" (Rajaram and Grundy-Warr 2004: 34).

[19] According to Pijpers and van Houtum, "[g]ated communities express a clear-cut form of socio-spatial insolidarity, of the purification of space, by shutting the gates for the 'outside' world under the flag of privacy, comfort and security. [...]. The gates of the gated community are not only a result of the desire to produce a space for the outsider, the stranger, but even more so, a purified space for the insider" (2005). In other words, the term describes this situation of "walls within walls" (Brown 2010) that we are witnessing at the beginning of the twenty-first century.

References

Amnesty International. 2015. "Greece: Farmakonisi Migrant Tragedy – One Year on and Still no Justice for Victims". https://www.amnesty.org/en/latest/news/2015/01/greece-farmakonisi-migrant-tragedy-one-year-and-still-no-justice-victims/ (Accessed 2 November 2017).

Amoore, L. and De Goede, M. 2005. "Governance, Risk and Dataveillance in the War on Terror". *Crime, Law & Social Change*, 43: 149–173. https://doi.org/10.1007/s10611-005-1717-8.

Anderson, B. 2006. *Imagined Communities. Reflections on the Origin and Spread of Nationalism*. London/New York: Verso.

Bigo, D. 2007. "Detention of Foreigners, States of Exception and the Social Practices of Control of the Banopticon". In P.K. Rajaram and C. Grundy-Warr (eds.), *Borderscapes. Hidden Geographies and Politics at Territory's Edge*. Minneapolis: University of Minnesota Press.

Bigo, D. 2008. "Globalized (In)security: the Field and the Ban-opticon". In D. Bigo and A. Tsoukala (eds.), *Terror, Insecurity and Liberty. Illiberal practices of liberal regimes after 9/11*. London/New York: Routledge.

Broeders, D. 2007. "The New Digital Borders of Europe: EU Databases and the Surveillance of Irregular Migrants". *International Sociology* 22: 71–92. https://doi.org/10.1177/0268580907070126.

Broeders, D. 2011. "A European 'Border' Surveillance System under Construction". In H. Dijstelbloem and A. Meijer (eds.), *Migration and the New Technological Borders of Europe*. Basingstoke, UK: Palgrave Macmillan.

Brown, W. 2010. *Walled States. Waning Sovereignty*. New York: Zone Books.

Butler, J. 2004. "Violence, Mourning, Politics". In *Precarious Life. The Powers of Mourning and Violence*. London/New York: Verso.

Carassava, A. and Aldrick, P. 2015. "We Cannot Keep Isis Out if EU Keeps Bullying Us, Says Greece". *The Times*, 7 April. https://www.thetimes.co.uk/article/we-cannot-keep-isis-out-if-eu-keeps-bullying-us-says-greece-wcdg0rbx0fn (Accessed 31 January 2016).

Christides, G. and Stefatou, O. (2017). "The Greek Island Camp Where Only the Sick or Pregnant Can Leave". *The Guardian*, 4 November. https://www.theguardian.com/world/2017/nov/04/the-greek-island-camp-where-only-the-sick-or-pregnant-can-leave (Accessed 8 November 2017).

Clarke, R.A. 1988. "Information Technology and Dataveillance". *Communications of the ACM*, 31(5): 498-512.

Council of Europe. 2016. "EU-Turkey Statement, 18 March 2016", 18 March. http://www.consilium.europa.eu/en/press/press-releases/2016/03/18/eu-turkey-statement/ (Accessed 2 November 2017).

Council of Europe. 2017. "Report to the Greek Government on the visits to Greece carried out by the European Committee for the Prevention of Torture and Inhuman or Degrading Treatment or Punishment (CPT) from 13 to 18 April and 19 to 25 July 2016", 26 September. http://www.politico.eu/wp-content/uploads/2017/09/CPT-report.pdf (Accessed 30 October 2017).

ERT International. 2017. "Effort to Winterise Hotspots Delayed Due to Lack of Space to Work, Mouzalas Tells ANA from Lesvos". http://int.ert.gr/effort-to-winterise-hotspots-delayed-due-to-lack-of-space-to-work-mouzalas-tells-ana-from-lesvos/ (Accessed 4 November 2017).

European Commission. 2011. "Press Release: EUROSUR: 'Connecting the Dots' in Border Surveillance", 12 December. http://europa.eu/rapid/press-release_IP-11-1528_en.htm (Accessed 30 October 2017).

European Commission. 2013. "Press Release: EUROSUR Kicks Off: New Tools to Save Migrants' Lives and Prevent Crime at EU Borders", 29 November. http://europa.eu/rapid/press-release_IP-13-1182_en.htm (Accessed 31 January 2016).

European Commission. 2016a. "Remarks by Commissioner Avramopoulos during His Visit to Idomeni, Greece", 15 March. http://europa.eu/rapid/press-release_SPEECH-16-828_en.htm (Accessed 30 October 2017).

European Commission. 2016b. "Fact Sheet: Managing the Refugee Crisis, EU-Turkey Statement", 4 October. http://europa.eu/rapid/press-release_MEMO-16-3218_en.pdf (Accessed 2 November 2017).

European Commission. 2016c. "Communication from the Commission to the European Parliament, the European Council and the Council. Back to Schengen – A Roadmap", 4 March. https://ec.europa.eu/home-affairs/sites/homeaffairs/files/what-we-do/policies/borders-and-visas/schengen/docs/communication-back-to-schengen-roadmap_en.pdf (Accessed 4 November 2017).

European Commission. 2017. "The Updated Schengen Rules". https://ec.europa.eu/home-affairs/sites/homeaffairs/files/what-we-do/policies/european-agenda-migration/20170927_factsheet_updated_schengen_rules_en.pdf (Accessed 4 November 2017).

European Parliament. 2013a. "Press Releases. EU Border Surveillance: MEPs Approve Eurosur Operating Rules", 10 October. http://www.europarl.europa.eu/news/en/news-room/20131007IPR21624/EU-border-surveillance-MEPs-approve-Eurosur-operating-rules (Accessed 20 January 2017).

European Parliament. 2013b. "German Press Review – 02 December 2013". http://www.europarl.europa.eu/germany/resource/static/files/ep_press_review_02.12.2013.pdf (Accessed 2 November 2017).

European Union. 2013. "Regulation (EU) No 1052/2013 of the European Parliament and of the Council of 22 October 2013 establishing the European Border Surveillance System (Eurosur)". *Official Journal of the European Union*, 6 November. http://frontex.europa.eu/assets/Legal_basis/Eurosur_Regulation_2013.pdf (Accessed 30 October 2017).

Fassin, D. 2007. "Humanitarianism as a Politics of Life", tr. R. Gomme. *Public Culture*, 19(3): 499–520. https://doi.org/10.1215/08992363-2007-007.

Filippidis, C. (2013). "Inventing Maps: Medical Police as Public Space Cartographer. I. 'The Abstract Nakedness of Being Human' – Modernity as Short-circuit", tr. A. Vradis. http://www.crisis-scape.net/blog/item/165-inventing-maps-medical-police-as-public-space-cartographer (Accessed 3 November 2017).

Foucault, M. 2006. *History of Madness*, tr. J. Murphy and J. Khalfa. London/New York: Routledge.

Grant, S. 2011. "Recording and Identifying European Frontier Deaths". *European Journal of Migration and Law*, 13: 135–156. https://doi.org/10.1163/157181611X571259.

Holehouse, M. and Fraser, I. 2015. "Migrant Crisis: European Council President Tusk Warns Schengen on Brink of Collapse". *The Telegraph*, 13 November. http://www.telegraph.co.uk/news/worldnews/europe/eu/11991098/Migrant-crisis-Donald-Tusk-warns-that-Schengen-is-on-brink-of-collapse-latest-news.html (Accessed 21 November 2015).

Home Office. 2007. "Securing the UK Border. Our Vision and Strategy for the Future". http://www.dematerialisedid.com/pdfs/Securing_the_UK_Border_final.pdf (Accessed 16 February 2016).

http://webtv.ert.gr/ert1/eidiseis/07mar2016-2100-deltio-idiseon/ [in Greek] (Accessed 31 October 2017).

http://webtv.ert.gr/category/ert1/eidiseis/news-prosfyges/ (Accessed 31 October 2017).

Khosravi, S. 2010. *'Illegal Traveller'. An Auto-Ethnography of Borders*. Basingstoke, UK: Palgrave Macmillan.

Last, T. and Spijkerboer, T. 2014. "Tracking Deaths in the Mediterranean". In T. Brian and F. Laczko (eds.), *Fatal Journeys. Tracking Lives Lost during Migration*. Geneva: International Organization for Migration.

Levi, M. and Wall, D.S. 2004. "Technologies, Security, and Privacy in the Post-9/11 European Information Society". *Journal of Law and Society*, 31(2): 194–220. http://www.academia.edu/26128622/Technologies_Security_and_Privacy_in_the_Post-9_11_European_Information_Society (Accessed 21 November 2017).

Lyon, D. 2005. "The Border is Everywhere: ID Cards, Surveillance and the Other". In E. Zureik and M.B. Salter (eds.), *Global Surveillance and Policing. Borders, Security, Identity*. Cullompton: Willan Publishing.

Mathiesen, T. 1999. *On Globalisation of Control: Towards an Integrated Surveillance System in Europe*. London: Statewatch Publication.

Mattei, U. 2010. "Emergency-Based Predatory Capitalism: The Rule of Law, Alternative Dispute Resolution, and Development". In D. Fassin and M. Pandolfi (eds.), *Contemporary States of Emergency. The Politics of Military and Humanitarian Interventions*. New York: Zone Books.

Médecins Sans Frontières. 2014. "Italy and the EU Must Not Abandon Refugees at Sea". http://www.msf.org/article/italy-and-eu-must-not-abandon-refugees-sea (Accessed 30 October 2017).

Open The Islands. 2017. "Joint Statement: Open The Islands – No More Dead from Cold!", 12 October. https://opentheislands.wordpress.com/statement/ (Accessed 30 October 2017).

Pandolfi, M. 2003. "Contract of Mutual (In)Difference: Government and the Humanitarian Apparatus in Contemporary Albania and Kosovo". *Indiana Journal of Global Legal Studies*, 10(1): 369–381. http://www.repository.law.indiana.edu/cgi/viewcontent.cgi?article=1259&context=ijgls (Accessed 10 September 2017).

Pandolfi, M. 2010. "From Paradox to Paradigm: The Permanent State of Emergency in the Balkans". In D. Fassin and M. Pandolfi (eds.), *Contemporary States of Emergency. The Politics of Military and Humanitarian Interventions.* New York: Zone Books.

Papadopoulos, D. and Tsianos, V. 2007. "The Autonomy of Migration: The Animals of Undocumented Mobility". In A. Hickey-Moody and P. Malins (eds.), *Deleuzian Encounters. Studies in Contemporary Social Issues.* Basingstoke, UK: Palgrave Macmillan.

Pijpers, R., van Houtum, H. 2005. "Towards a Gated Community". *Eurozine.* http://www.eurozine.com/articles/2005-01-12-houtumpijpers-en.html (Accessed 23 January 2016).

Pope Francis. 2013. Twitter, 12 October. https://twitter.com/pontifex/status/388978829043068929 (Accessed 12 October 2013).

Rajaram K.P., and Grundy-Warr, C. 2004. "The Irregular Migrant as Homo Sacer: Migration and Detention in Australia, Malaysia, and Thailand". *International Migration*, 42(1): 33–63. https://doi.org/10.1111/j.0020-7985.2004.00273.x.

RSA. 2017. "Winter has Arrived: Thousands Left at the Mercy of Winter in Greek Hot-spots", 25 October. http://rsaegean.org/winter-has-arrived-thousands-left-at-the-mercy-of-winter-in-greek-hot-spots/ (Accessed 30 October 2017).

Sidaway, J.D. 2007. "The Poetry of Boundaries". In P.K. Rajaram and C. Grundy-Warr (eds.), *Borderscapes. Hidden Geographies and Politics at Territory's Edge.* Minneapolis: University of Minnesota Press.

SigmaLive. 2015. "EU Border Agency Urges Stronger Barriers", 5 October. http://www.sigmalive.com/en/news/international/135893/eu-border-agency-urges-stronger-barriers (Accessed 4 November 2017).

Sitaropoulos, N. 2017. "Migrant III – Treatment in Greek Law Enforcement – Are the Strasbourg Court Judgments the Tip of the Iceberg?". https://papers.ssrn.com/sol3/papers.cfm?abstract_id=2921109 (Accessed 13 December 2017).

Smith, H. 2016. "Refugee Bottleneck in Greece Leads to Warning of Humanitarian Crisis". *The Guardian*, 6 March. https://www.theguardian.com/world/2016/

mar/06/growing-refugee-bottleneck-greece-warning-humanitarian-crisis (Accessed 30 October 2017).
Sunderland, J. 2014. "Dispatches: Honor Lampedusa's Dead by Sustaining Boat Rescue". https://www.hrw.org/news/2014/10/02/dispatches-honor-lampedusas-dead-sustaining-boat-rescue (Accessed 20 January 2016).
Tsipras, A. 2016. Twitter, 24 March. https://twitter.com/PrimeministerGR/status/713028715366785026?ref_src=twsrc%5Etfw&ref_url=http%3A%2F%2Fwww.ert.gr%2Feidiseis%2Fellada%2Faravofono-deltio-ert-chrisimes-idisis-ke-plirofories-gia-tous-prosfiges-vid%2F (Accessed 3 November 2017).
Utas, M. 2005. "Victimcy, Girlfriending, Soldiering: Tactic Agency in a Young Woman's Social Navigation of the Liberian War Zone". *Anthropological Quarterly*, 78(2): 403–430. https://doi.org/10.1353/anq.2005.0032.
Vaughan-Williams, N. 2009. *Border Politics. The Limits of Sovereign Power*. Edinburgh: Edinburgh University Press.
Walters, W. 2006. "Rethinking Borders Beyond the State". *Comparative European Politics*, 4: 141–159. https://doi.org/10.1057/palgrave.cep.6110076.

CHAPTER 5

Borders and Bodies in Twenty-First-Century Biopolitical Societies: The Migrant's Body as Carrier of the Border

Abstract Within the new digital borders of Europe and the introduction of biometrics in migration control and management, the human body has received a greater significance and has become the *par excellence* border. This chapter focuses on the migrant's body as carrier of limitations, dichotomies and borders, and, consequently, on the examination of the functions of racism within the frame of twenty-first-century biopolitical societies.

Keywords Human body • Biopolitical power • Biopolitical societies • Biometrics • Racism • Foucault

Within the frame of the intensifying militarisation of control and surveillance mechanisms, the human body has emerged in the forefront, as it becomes manifest, among others, through the intensification and regularisation of the use of biometrics. Without doubt, this systematic, scientific interest in the body does not constitute a novel procedure, but can be traced back to the eighteenth century, within the disciplinary mechanisms of the body that Michel Foucault called "anatomo-politics of the human body" and the regulatory mechanisms of the population he called "biopolitics of the population" (1998, 2003). In other words, through the co-articulation of technologies of surveillance and regulation, within the specific historical conditions of capitalism's consolidation, the body—

T. Lagios et al., *Borders, Bodies and Narratives of Crisis in Europe*,
https://doi.org/10.1007/978-3-319-75586-1_5

individual and collective—and all its parameters were transformed into the *par excellence* object of a nexus of systematic scientific knowledge and power relations. Thus, the focal point of this novel biopolitical power became "the 'body politic', as a set of material elements and techniques that serve as weapons, relays, communication routes and supports for the power and knowledge relations that invest human bodies and subjugate them by turning them into objects of knowledge" (Foucault 1991: 28).

Since the consolidation of neoliberal societies in the 1970s, the body acquired a greater significance and centrality; through the steady molecularisation of life, the emphasis upon the optimisation of life and the new modes of subjectification, "human beings come to experience themselves in new ways as biological creatures, as biological selves, their vital existence becomes a focus of government, the target of novel forms of authority and expertise, a highly cathected field for knowledge, an expanding territory for bioeconomic exploitation, an organising principle of ethics, and the stake in a molecular vital politics" (Rose 2007: 4).[1] Thus, new forms of citizenship and new modes of subjectivity are now emerging in reference to the body itself; the ethical, prudential, respectable citizen is now the healthy, self-disciplined, self-governing subject. Within the new digital technologies of control and management, the body is being also conceived, analysed and confronted "as a source of information, the code of which can be read by a machine" and, equally, as an "information storage device that simply has to be scanned in order to be registered" (Dijstelbloem et al. 2011: 12)[2]; in other words, the body, the "surface of the inscription of events",[3] becomes the necessary password for every recognisable and viable identity within contemporary societies of control.

Firstly, it should be highlighted that "[i]n the biomarkets of neo-liberal governance in the new millennium, the idea of health threats are being

[1] See, also Rose and Novas (2005). For a review of Rose's major work *The Politics of Life Itself: Biomedicine, Power, and Subjectivity in the Twenty-First Century*, see Lekka (2013a).

[2] For Van der Ploeg, this has led to the emergence of a new ontology of the body: "[t]hrough these partly connecting and overlapping technological practices, then, a new body ontology is emerging, that redefines bodies in terms of, or even as, information" (2003: 64).

[3] In Foucault's words: "The body is the surface of the inscription of events (traced by language and dissolved by ideas), the locus of the dissociation of Me (to which it tries to impart the chimera of a substantial unity), and a volume in perpetual disintegration. Genealogy, as an analysis of descent, is thus situated within the articulation of the body and history. Its task is to expose a body totally imprinted by history and the process of history's destruction of the body" (2000: 375–376).

increasingly used in the re-construction of both borders and the idea of what constitutes rightful citizenship" (Harper and Raman 2008: 8); but, let us keep in mind that the notion of citizenship itself constitutes "a form of governance which performs and reproduces *exclusion* and not inclusion" (Trimikliniotis et al. 2015: 28; emphasis added). Within this context, the dominant rhetoric regarding migration, as it is the case with any other "dangerous" population groups, is systematically articulated through medicine's discourse, leading to the creation of moral panic through the representation of migrants' bodies as possible carriers of "dangerous" diseases and as infectious "miasmas" vis-à-vis the healthy citizens of the body politic.[4] It is noteworthy that European borders' closing in 2015 was accompanied by the gradual introduction of articles in the press concerning "migrants' diseases", always under the disguise of unselfish interest and humanism.[5] Using as a pretext the health of the body politic, "[t]he rhetoric of anti-immigration was expanded through a language that was explicitly medical, and paranoia about 'racial others' was reconstituted as policy on 'public health'" (Harper and Raman 2008: 8). Undoubtedly, this "integration of medicine and politics" (Agamben 1998: 143) and the concomitant dichotomy between "normal" and "pathological" bodies[6] are not inventions of twenty-first-century societies. Instead, they constitute one of the

[4]As Mary Douglas underlines, "[m]iasma is an instrument of total rejection. The mere physical presence of the unwanted Other is dangerous. Their use of the same space and times and their breathing the common air is a menace to the rest of the community" (1994: 114–115). A quite characteristic example of the medicalisation of "Otherness" was the hunger strike of 300 migrants in Greece, on 25 January 2011. Demanding the recognition of their status as political refugees, 300 migrants decided to go on hunger strike to fight against their inhumane living conditions. The occupation of the building of the Law School, at the University of Athens, by migrants and activists supporting their fight, raised a storm of reactions within Greek society. It is indicative that most reactions did not focus on migrants' demands, but on the supposed "risks" that their "infectious" bodies were posing to public health. In other words, the debate was articulated primarily in biomedical terms; the Greek society seemed to face a public health crisis, whereas Andreas Loverdos, Minister of Health, introduced then the term "hygienic bomb" into the public debate to describe the migrants' resisting bodies.

[5]An indicative example is the article "Which are the refugees' diseases", published in the online edition of *Kathimerini*, one of the most reputable Greek newspapers, on 28 February 2016 (Mpouloutza 2016).

[6]At this point, let us keep in mind that "[t]o set a norm (*normer*), to normalize, is to impose a requirement on an existence, a given whose variety, disparity, with regard to the requirement, present themselves as a hostile, even more than unknown, indeterminant. It is, in effect, a *polemical* concept [...]" (Canguilhem 1991: 239; emphasis added).

essential characteristics of biopolitical power, following a well-established historical tradition in Western societies towards every "abnormal"; from the "Great Confinement" in the seventeenth century (Foucault 2006) to the quarantine in the eighteenth-century pestilent cities and the measures against epidemics (Foucault 1991; Foucault 2007), to the measures against the "dangerous classes" in the nineteenth century, up to the lives "unworthy of life" in Nazi concentration camps. At the beginning of the twenty-first century, the notion of "risk"[7] is constitutive of the dominant medical discourse, leading to the control, normalisation and exclusion of those population groups deemed as "threatening" and "dangerous" for public health; for, "[t]hose deemed to be 'a risk' or 'at risk' are vulnerable to having their freedoms curtailed, be subject to close monitoring, ostracism (e.g. deportation) or in some cases physical restrained [...]" (Petersen and Wilkinson 2008: 8).[8] From this perspective, we are witnessing a systematic attempt towards the medicalisation of migration, its displacement from the field of politics to that of science and, consequently, its management as another technocratic, non-political matter;[9] at the same time, "to liken a political event or situation to an illness is to impute guilt, to prescribe punishment" (Sontag 1978: 83).

Under this prism, biometrics, one of the ten breakthrough technologies for 2001 according to *MIT Technology Review*,[10] has received a central place and normative status in the control, management and identification of the human body and, consequently, in the construction of migrants' identity. A 2005 technical report by the European Commission underlines that "[b]iometric technologies provide a strong mechanism for authentication and therefore can promote the development of a 'trusted' Information Society" and, more importantly, "increase security and the

[7] On the concept of "risk", see Beck (2007); Luhmann (1993); Lupton (1999).

[8] To this direction, quite indicative is the common attitude towards migrants in camps, hotspots and detention centres, in reference to migrants' eating habits, personal hygiene and behaviour deemed as "risky" and "dangerous". As it is asserted by Scott-Smith in his interesting study on the supplementary feeding programme in a camp in South Sudan, "[t]here was little space to acknowledge that people's existing behaviour may make sense where they come from, or that there might be something to learn from local beliefs. What was left was a clear sense of correct and incorrect action, bound up with a discourse of civilized and uncivilized conduct" (2014: 31).

[9] Besides, "[t]he very notion of 'management' is characterized by its apolitical and technocratic nature, and its popularity (to the detriment of other notions such as 'the politics of migration') is in itself a way of depoliticizing migration" (Geiger and Pécoud 2010: 11).

[10] See, http://www2.technologyreview.com/tr10/?year=2001.

sense of security", whereas one of their main advantages is that "[s]ince a person's biometric features are a part of his or her body, they will always be with that person where ever he/she goes and available to prove his or her identity" (2005: 97, 11). Even though we could claim that the use of the body as a source of identification has indeed a long history, dating back, at least, to nineteenth-century anthropometry and fingerprinting within the frame of the consolidation of biopolitical societies,[11] the twenty-first-century introduction of biometrics, "a technology firmly enmeshed within relations of *biopower*" (Pugliese 2010: 1; emphasis in the original), has led to a series of highly significant implications and consequences.

In essence, the first attempt to introduce and record biometrics in migration control and management dates back in 1997, with the introduction of the European Dactylographic System (EURODAC) that was designed for the implementation of the 1990 Dublin Convention, that is, the co-operation of member-states for the examination of the applications for asylum (European Union 1997). EURODAC, which began its operation in 2003, was "the very first common Automated Fingerprint Identification System (AFIS) within the European Union" (European Commission 2013) for the registration of the digital fingerprints of every person over the age of 14 who has applied for asylum in an EU country.[12] Since then, there has appeared a series of systems for the recognition of iris and facial patterns, DNA profiling, heartbeat detection and age assessment,[13] to name but a few. And, in 2016 even an iris scan payment system has been introduced in three refugee camps in Jordan (King Abdullah Park, Azraq, Za'atari) by the World Food Programme (WFP), in collaboration with UNHCR; this system allows refugees to purchase food from camp supermarkets by using a scan of their eyes instead of cash or any other means of payment (UN News Centre 2016).

Within the context of these new "biometric" borders, the human body is transformed into the *par excellence* carrier of limits, borders and dichotomies; for, "the biometric border is the portable border par excellence, carried by mobile bodies at the very same time as it is deployed to divide bodies at international boundaries, airports, railway stations, on subways

[11] It is characteristic that, for Pugliese, "[b]iometrics, in one form or another, has been deployed in human societies for millennia" (2010: 26). See, also Ajana (2013); Lyon (2008).

[12] On EURODAC and the introduction of biometrics, see also Van der Ploeg (1999); Ceyhan (2008); Ajana (2013).

[13] Extremely interesting is the recent report on age assessment published by the Council of Europe (2017).

or city streets, in the office or the neighbourhood" (Amoore 2006: 338), leading, at the same time, to the continuous dissolution and re-inscription of established dichotomies. Quite indicative is the discussion about the so-called smart borders that consist in travellers' identification in Europe and the USA, through, among others, the recognition of iris and facial patterns; of course, this applies to those "citizens" who have been given the opportunity to travel all over the world for business, studies or pleasure, always with the obligation to carry the necessary biometric passport, and whose body temporarily possesses the "trusted traveller biometrics".[14] For Agamben, "by applying these techniques and these devices invented for the dangerous classes to a citizen, or rather to a human being as such, states [...] have made the person the ideal suspect, to the point that it's humanity itself that has become the dangerous class" (2004). Through a constant procedure of exhaustive surveillance, recording in vast databases and assessment based upon specific criteria, "a state of conscious and permanent visibility" is imposed, enabling "the automatic function of power" (Foucault 1991: 201).

From the aforementioned, it becomes evident that through the dominant technoscientific practices, enunciations and "innovations" regarding the human body, "every person of 'irregular presence' on EU territory", as well as outside the European territory, "when asked for identification, may be required to have their body read by a sensor able to detect the mark of *illegality*" (Van der Ploeg 1999: 301; emphasis added). In other words, the concept of the border is "always in the act of becoming", in a continuous search "for proof of status and legitimacy" (Amoore 2006: 348). Hence, it does not refer exclusively to national or international borders, territorial waters and fences, databases and digital means, but intrudes into and is seated in, on and around the body, its mobility and the spaces where it is allowed and legitimised to move; for Vaughan-Williams, it is this concept of the "generalized biopolitical border" that "points to the

[14] In any case, there is still a clear distinction between the legitimisation and security offered by the trusted traveller biometrics and the constant surveillance and control implied by the migrant biometrics: "Whereas the *trusted traveller biometrics* tend to emphasize membership of (or inclusion in) a group based on pre-screening checks such as citizenship and past travel patterns, what I will call *immigrant biometrics* are based on ongoing surveillance and checks on patterns of behaviour. While for the trusted traveller the biometric submission is usually the end of the matter, the passport to 'borders lite' (if not to a borderless world), the risky traveller's biometric submission is only the beginning of a world of perennial dataveillance where the border looms large" (Amoore 2006: 343; emphasis in the original).

way in which bordering practices are rather more diffused throughout society than the modern geopolitical imaginary implies" (2009: 117). Thus, the human body becomes the border *per se* that, depending on its distinguishing features, has inscribed in itself its imminent inclusion or its imminent exclusion. Bodies are now displaced, confined or excluded, depending on the forms, the spaces and the limits of their own mobility and, consequently, their own presence, revealing, at the same time, the contradictions and limitations of Western democracy (Benhabib 2004); namely, a "[d]emocracy for an insignificant minority, democracy for the rich – that is the democracy of capitalist society" (Lenin 2014: 125).

As a result, the constant re-inscription of demarcation lines between "natives" and "foreigners", "legal" and "illegal", "migrants" and "refugees", "normal" and "pathological" is, in fact, a constitutive condition of biopolitical societies. Through this procedure, it is eventually the human body—and, first and foremost, the migrant's body—within and through which the exception "is realized *normally*" (Agamben 1998: 170; emphasis in the original). There is constructed a specific identity of the migrant who becomes non-viable and to whom a new social and political substance is attributed; it is the identity of the "man without qualities", of the "non-citizen",[15] of the life deemed as "unworthy of life". At the beginning of the twenty-first century, migrants are, in fact, stripped off any political substance and human quality, bringing to mind the "Muselmann" of Nazi concentration camps who also signified "the moving threshold in which man passed into non-man" (Agamben 1999: 47).[16] Under the prism of twenty-first-century biopolitical power, the exception is imposed through the compulsory recording of personal and biometric data; through compulsory medical examinations[17] and compulsory vaccinations,

[15] It is indicative that the loss of citizenship is called "denaturalization", that is, *inter alia*, becoming "unnatural": "[c]itizenship has become the *nature* of being human. Being outside the realm of citizenship means being outside nature" (Khosravi 2010: 122; emphasis in the original).

[16] In the camps' slang, the "Muselmann" was the detainee, who had given up any hope and literally given up himself/herself, living on the threshold between life and death (Agamben 1999).

[17] In Greece, the events that took place in April 2012 were rather characteristic. A few days before the national elections of May 2012, police proceeded to mass adductions of prostitutes. Twelve women, initially presented by politicians and journalists as "migrants" and "illegal prostitutes", were medically examined without their consent and found seropositive to HIV virus. This had as a result their arrest, their debasement through the publication of their photos in the media and their imprisonment for more than eight months, even though

as we recently witnessed in Idomeni camp and elsewhere;[18] through the compulsory confinement in camps and detention centres. Faced with this impasse, hunger strike and suicide are often considered by migrants as the only response towards a biopolitical power that historically defends the undeniable, ultimate value only of those lives deemed as "worthy of life".

And if we are now wondering how it is possible, almost a century after the publication of the book by Hoche and Binding, entitled *Permitting the Destruction of Life Unworthy of Life* (*Die Freigabe der Vernichtung lebensunwerten Lebens*, 1920), which had been the "bible" of the Nazi rhetoric and practices,[19] to still witness dichotomies between lives deemed as "worthy of life" and lives deemed as "unworthy of life", the answer is to be found in the historical function and targeting of biopolitical power. In order to interpret the devaluation and annihilation of human life through the mechanisms and functions of a power that is supposed to focus on the enhancement and security of this life, the key word that emerges is *racism*. For, it is the rhetoric and practices of racism that have paved the path through which the sovereign "power of life and death" could penetrate into the disciplinary/regulatory system of biopolitical power (Foucault 2003). According to Foucault's analytics, there are two basic functions of racism, which are clearly highlighted in what we have already described regarding migration control and management. First, there are constantly

they were eventually acquitted. The main issue was the "danger" to public health that their "miasmatic" bodies were posing, whereas the Minister of Health Andreas Loverdos was once again speaking of "hygienic bombs", ordering the expansion of medical control under the pretext of the security of the "Greek family".

[18] In May 2016, systematic vaccinations began in Idomeni and other camps all over Greece. These vaccinations followed the reactions of a significant part of the Greek society against refugees' children who were going to attend Greek schools. Many Greek parents were claiming that refugees' children were carrying diseases that were going to infect Greek children, demanding the immediate vaccination of refugees' children.

[19] Alfred Hoche (1865–1943) was professor of psychiatry and director of the psychiatric clinic at the University of Freiburg, and Karl Binding (1841–1920) was law professor at the University of Leipzig. In their book *Permitting the Destruction of Life Unworthy of Life*, they were openly in favour of the extermination of all lives deemed as "unworthy of life", legitimising, in this way, "euthanasia". Their ideas culminated in the sterilisation programme during the period 1933–1939, where more than 400,000 mentally and physically ill persons were subjected to compulsory sterilisation, and the "euthanasia programme", known as "Aktion T4", during the period 1939–1945, where more than 100,000 mental patients, along with other groups of mentally and physically ill individuals, were killed by Nazi doctors in gas chambers, through poison injections and through forced food deprivation. See, Burleigh (1991); Lekka (2013b).

imposed demarcation lines on the biological and, consequently, social continuum, consolidating the dichotomy between lives "worthy of life" and lives "unworthy of life"—through either borders/fences, or even human bodies themselves. Second, in direct correlation to the first function, the life and security of the first is directly connected with the death of the latter. And, given that, as we have already underlined, death is not a univocal concept and does not refer exclusively to "simply murder as such, but also every form of indirect murder: the fact of exposing someone to death, increasing the risk of death for some people, or, quite simply, political death, expulsion, rejection, and so on" (ibid: 256), it turns out that the dominant technologies of control, surveillance and exclusion of migrants' bodies could be regarded as a constituent element of racism in twenty-first-century biopolitical societies. In this way, the biopolitics of migration turns out to be, eventually, the "management of *non-life*" or, equally, the "(mis)management of *death*" (Ajana 2013: 58; emphasis in the original).

By taking into consideration the above parameters, it becomes clear that Western societies' exclusion of every "Other" does not constitute an "anomaly" or an "exception", but a constitutive condition of their own "normality" and "rule"; as Agamben underlines, "*[t]he rule applies to the exception in no longer applying, in withdrawing from it*" (1998: 18; emphasis in the original). In other words, it is not just about a state-organised racism or a racism expressed by an extreme right party—as it is the common doxa; instead, it is about a constituent element of biopolitical societies orbiting around the body itself. And, as soon as the established limits of the political are threatened to be displaced and the first voices of resistance are echoing by migrants, as well as any other "vulnerable" population group and all those people who are, in one way or another, in solidarity with them, then, by following a long historical tradition, the established power relations are displaced once again towards "repressive legislation and government by the sword" (Kropotkin 1995: 18).

References

Agamben, G. 1998. *Homo Sacer. Sovereign Power and Bare Life*, tr. D. Heller-Roazen. Stanford, CA: Stanford University Press.

Agamben, G. 1999. *Remnants of Auschwitz. The Witness and the Archive*, tr. D. Heller-Roazen. New York: Zone Books.

Agamben, G. 2004. "No to Bio-Political Tattooing". *Le Monde*, 10 January. http://www.ratical.org/ratville/CAH/totalControl.html (Accessed 29 January 2014).

Ajana, B. 2013. *Governing through Biometrics. The Biopolitics of Identity*. Basingstoke, UK: Palgrave Macmillan.

Amoore, L. 2006. "Biometric Borders: Governing Mobilities in the War on Terror". *Political Geography* 25: 336–351. https://doi.org/10.1016/j.polgeo.2006.02.001.

Beck, U. 2007. *Risk Society. Towards a New Modernity*. London: SAGE Publications.

Benhabib, S. 2004. *The Rights of Others. Aliens, Residents and Citizens*. Cambridge: Cambridge University Press.

Burleigh, M. 1991. "Racism as Social Policy: The Nazi 'Euthanasia' Programme, 1939–1945". *Ethnic and Racial Studies*, 14(4): 453–473.

Canguilhem, G. 1991. *The Normal and the Pathological*. New York: Zone Books.

Ceyhan, A. 2008. "Technologization of Security: Management of Uncertainty and Risk in the Age of Biometrics". *Surveillance & Society* 5(2): 102–123. https://queens.scholarsportal.info/ojs-archive/index.php/surveillance-and-society/article/viewFile/3430/3393 (Accessed 5 May 2017).

Council of Europe. 2017. "Age Assessment: Council of Europe Member States' Policies, Procedures and Practices Respectful of Children's Rights in the Context of Migration". https://rm.coe.int/age-assessment-council-of-europe-member-states-policies-procedures-and/168074b723 (Accessed 24 September 2017).

Dijstelbloem, H., Meijer, A., and Besters, M. 2011. "The Migration Machine". In H. Dijstelbloem and A. Meijer (eds.), *Migration and the New Technological Borders of Europe*. Basingstoke, UK: Palgrave Macmillan.

Douglas, M. 1994. *Risk and Blame. Essays in Cultural Theory*. London/New York: Routledge.

European Commission. 2005. "Biometrics at the Frontiers: Assessing the Impact on Society". http://ftp.jrc.es/EURdoc/eur21585en.pdf (Accessed 6 November 2017).

European Commission. 2013. "Press Release: Identification of Asylum Seekers – EURODAC Operational Tomorrow", 14 January. http://europa.eu/rapid/press-release_IP-03-37_en.htm (Accessed 6 November 2017).

European Union. 1997. "Convention Determining the State Responsible for Examining Applications for Asylum Lodged in One of the Member States of the European Communities (97/C 254/01)". *Official Journal of the European Communities*, 19 August. http://eur-lex.europa.eu/legal-content/EN/TXT/PDF/?uri=CELEX:41997A0819(01)&from=EN (Accessed 7 October 2017).

Foucault, M. 1991. *Discipline and Punish. The Birth of the Prison*, tr. A. Sheridan. London/New York: Penguin Books.

Foucault, M. 1998. *The History of Sexuality. Volume 1. The Will to Knowledge*, tr. R. Hurley. London/New York: Penguin Books.

Foucault, M. 2000. "Nietzsche, Genealogy, History". In J.D. Faubion (ed.), *Essential Works of Foucault 1954-1984. Volume 2. Aesthetics*, tr. R. Hurley and others. London/New York: Penguin Books.

Foucault, M. 2003. *"Society Must Be Defended". Lectures at the Collège de France, 1975-76*, tr. D. Macey. New York: Picador.

Foucault, M. 2006. *History of Madness*, tr. J. Murphy and J. Khalfa. London/New York: Routledge.

Foucault, M. 2007. *Security, Territory, Population, Lectures at the Collège de France, 1977–1978*, tr. G. Burchell. New York: Palgrave Macmillan.

Geiger, M. and Pécoud, A. 2010. "The Politics of International Migration Management". In M. Geiger and A. Pécoud (eds.), *The Politics of International Migration Management*. Basingstoke, UK: Palgrave Macmillan.

Harper, I. and Raman, P. 2008. "Less than Human? Diaspora, Disease and the Question of Citizenship". *International Migration*, 46(5): 3–26. https://doi.org/10.1111/j.1468-2435.2008.00486.x.

http://www2.technologyreview.com/tr10/?year=2001 (Accessed 6 November 2017).

Khosravi, S. 2010. *'Illegal Traveller'. An Auto-Ethnography of Borders*. Basingstoke, UK: Palgrave Macmillan.

Kropotkin, P. 1995. "The Conquest of Bread". In M.S. Shatz (ed.), *The Conquest of Bread and Other Writings*. New York: Cambridge University Press.

Lekka, V. 2013a. "Review of Nikolas Rose's *The Politics of Life Itself: Biomedicine, Power, and Subjectivity in the Twenty-First Century*". *Historein*, 13: 107–111. https://ejournals.epublishing.ekt.gr/index.php/historein/article/view/2270 (Accessed 6 November 2017).

Lekka, V. 2013b. "Psychiatry's Abuses: The Crimes of Nazi Germany" [in Greek]. https://uoa.academia.edu/VasiaLekka (Accessed 28 March 2016).

Lenin, V.I. 2014. *State and Revolution*, tr. T. Chretien. Chicago, IL: Haymarket Books.

Luhmann, N. 1993. *Risk: A Sociological Theory*. New York: A. de Gruyter.

Lupton, D. 1999. *Risk*. London/New York: Routledge.

Lyon, D. 2008. "Biometrics, Identification and Surveillance". *Bioethics*, 22(9): 499–508. https://doi.org/10.1111/j.1467-8519.2008.00697.x.

Mpouloutza, P. 2016. "Which are the Refugees' Diseases" [in Greek]. *Kathimerini*, 28 February. http://www.kathimerini.gr/851279/article/epikairothta/ellada/apo-ti-as8enoyn-oi-prosfyges (Accessed 2 March 2016).

Petersen, A. and Wilkinson, I. 2008. "Health, Risk and Vulnerability. An Introduction". In A. Petersen and I. Wilkinson (eds.), *Health, Risk and Vulnerability*. London/New York: Routledge.

Pugliese, J. 2010. *Biometrics. Bodies, Technologies, Biopolitics*. London/New York: Routledge.

Rose, N. and Novas, C. 2005. "Biological Citizenship". In A. Ong and S.J. Collier (eds.), *Global Assemblages. Technology, Politics and Ethics as Anthropological Problems.* Malden, MA: Blackwell Publishing.

Rose, N. 2007. *The Politics of Life Itself: Biomedicine, Power, and Subjectivity in the Twenty-First Century.* Princeton/Oxford: Princeton University Press.

Scott-Smith, T. 2014. "Control and Biopower in Contemporary Humanitarian Aid: The Case of Supplementary Feeding". *Journal of Refugee Studies,* 28(1): 21–37. https://doi.org/10.1093/jrs/feu018.

Sontag, S. 1978. *Illness as Metaphor.* New York: Farrar, Straus and Giroux.

Trimikliniotis, N., Parsanoglou, D., and Tsianos, V.S. 2015. *Mobile Commons, Migrant Digitalities and the Right to the City.* Basingstoke, UK: Palgrave Macmillan.

UN News Centre. 2016. "Iris Scan Helps Syrian Refugees in Jordan Receive UN Supplies in 'Blink of Eye'". http://www.un.org/apps/news/story.asp?NewsID=55223#.WgB_bXZLfIU (Accessed 6 November 2017).

Van der Ploeg, I. 1999. "The Illegal Body: 'Eurodac' and the Politics of Biometric Identification". *Ethics and Information Technology,* 1(4): 295–302. https://doi.org/10.1023/A:1010064613240.

Van der Ploeg, I. 2003. "Biometrics and the Body as Information: Normative Issues of the Socio-technical Coding of the Body". In D. Lyon (ed.), *Surveillance as Social Sorting. Privacy, Risk, and Digital Discrimination.* London/New York: Routledge.

Vaughan-Williams, N. 2009. *Border Politics. The Limits of Sovereign Power.* Edinburgh: Edinburgh University Press.

CHAPTER 6

Conclusion: Facing a Circulus Vitiosus?

Abstract This chapter focuses on the presentation of the conclusions of Part I of the book. Having as a point of departure some 2017 key events in relation to migration, this chapter aims at delineating the basic deductions of Part I through a series of questions and critical assumptions.

Keywords Migrants • Neoliberal societies • Resistance • Anti-politics

In January 2017, Donald Trump took office as the 45th President of the United States, after his win in the presidential elections that took place in November 2016, having as his target, among others, to crack down migration; in September 2017, the nationalist, right-wing populist Alternative für Deutschland (AfD) entered the Bundestag as the third party with 12.6% of the vote in the German federal elections, having migration literally at the centre of its election campaign; in November 2017, a Greek fascist group attacked the house of Amir, an 11-year-old boy from Afghanistan, a few days after a dispute over Amir's right to carry the Greek flag during a national holiday school parade in Athens.

Faced with this outbreak of extreme right-wing policies, xenophobic reactions and racist attacks against migrants; faced with the intensifying "rationalisation" of migration management and control through the

T. Lagios et al., *Borders, Bodies and Narratives of Crisis in Europe*,
https://doi.org/10.1007/978-3-319-75586-1_6

dichotomy between "refugees" and "migrants", and the concomitant exploitation of the most useful bodies for capitalism; faced with the consolidation of a military-humanitarian nexus to deal with the "humanist crisis", that reinforces not only migrants' exploitation, but, equally, their victimisation and exclusion as "invisible" non-subjects; faced with borders' transformation and diffusion to every cell of the body politic; faced with the continuous re-inscription of demarcation lines between lives "worthy of life" and lives "unworthy of life", it is quite reasonable to wonder if we could eventually escape from this impasse. In other words, the question that arises is if we could avoid this *circulus vitiosus*, given this *prima facie* "paradox" and puzzling "contradiction" of a society that hastens to renounce and condemn the barbarity of previous historical periods at the exact same time that it consolidates apparently less barbarous and more "civilized" conditions—as it is migrants' drowning in the Aegean Sea or their confinement in hotspots and camps—for every person who does not conform to its established norms; given that, as in Nazi concentration camps, so today "[t]he personages in these pages are not men. Their humanity is buried, or they themselves buried it, under the abuse received or inflicted on someone else" (Levi 2015: 166). Thus, how could we, actually, endure to be once again witnesses of another bloody event in the history of Western societies; namely, of the fact that eventually "[t]here is no document of civilization which is not at the same time a document of barbarism" (Benjamin 2007: 256)?

Our purpose has been, in no case, either to give answers and "solutions" or to try to speak on behalf of all those who experience daily exclusion, marginalisation and racism, namely, on behalf of all those whose life's prevailing condition is a state of exploitation, violence and constant precariousness. It is for this reason that we do not want to adopt the arrogant, often Orientalist trend of Western charity and the humanist discourse of its main exponents—international organisations and NGOs, politicians and journalists, or even activists—who assume a rather painless, collective responsibility of the West and express feelings of supposed "shame" and "guilt", confronting migrants as "helpless victims need protection, need someone to speak for them" (Malkki 1996: 388). On the contrary, living in an extremely critical historical conjuncture, given that neoliberalism does not constitute exclusively a system of economic governance, but, primarily, a biopolitical rationality of governance that produces and promotes specific exceptions for the exclusion of populations and the securing of social safety (Ong 2006), it is finally time to dare to remain silent in order to reflect on our position and stance towards migrants and to give the floor to migrants, but also to every "Other", who, by "speaking louder than any stone" (LGBTQI Refugees GR 2017), remind us of all the things we easily repress to oblivion, namely, of the "tradition of the oppressed", that should, after all, remind us that "we are all members of the community of the governed, and thereby obliged to show mutual solidarity" (Foucault 2002: 474).

If, in fact, "[i]t is more pleasant and useful to go through the 'experience of revolution' than to write about it" (Lenin 2014: 165), our purpose has been to delineate the political, social, ideological and epistemological implications of migration control and management in twenty-first-century Western societies, in order to highlight the necessity to invent new forms, means and points of resistance, not through the invocation of another "grand narrative" about the past and possibly the future, but in the "hic et nunc" of the present. Besides, "[t]hese points of resistance are present everywhere in the power network. Hence there is no single locus of great Refusal, no soul of revolt, source of all rebellions, or pure law of the revolutionary. Instead there is a plurality of resistances [...]" (Foucault 1998: 95–96).

In sum, within a neoliberal society that, under the pretext of another financial, political and humanist "crisis", has imposed a permanent "state of emergency", it is migrants' bodies, along with other population groups, that have become the *par excellence* object of a biopolitical power that erects borders, limits and walls, transforming them into "bare lives" in twenty-first-century Western societies; but, after all, "'[b]are life' is never obtained, [...]. It is the political dream of some bearers of power" (Bigo 2007: 12). It is these borders, limits and walls that are rapidly multiplying, dissolving the dominant dichotomies and intruding into the body even of those lives deemed as "worthy of life", for the security of whom they were supposedly erected in the first place. And it is exactly these borders, limits and walls that should be decisively challenged in their materiality, changing, first and foremost, the mentalities and behaviours that breed and sustain them. Thus, following Foucault, we should actually keep in mind the fact that politics is eventually the continuation of war with other means.[1]

[1] According to Carl von Clausewitz, "[d]er Krieg ist eine bloße Fortsetzung der Politik mit anderen Mitteln" ("War is a bare continuation of politics with other means") (2003: 27). Reversing Clausewitz's phrase, Foucault wrote: "It may be that war as strategy is a continuation of politics. But it must not be forgotten that 'politics' has been conceived as a continu-

For, how else could we describe, among others, the shipwrecks in the Aegean Sea and migrants' confrontation in Idomeni camp and elsewhere, if not as a violent, bloody and interminable war? All in all, it is, at last, time to raise these questions, trying to articulate alternative *discourses* and invent new forms of *anti-politics* against a condition so desperate that eventually can only fill us with hope.[2] And if we still have the illusion that this struggle is taking place somewhere else, far away from our "worthy of life" lives and our "borderless" world, we should always keep in mind Marx's warning to his readers in the preface to the first edition of the *Capital* in 1867: "*De te fabula narratur!*" (Marx 1976: 90).

References

Benjamin, W. 2007. "Theses on the Philosophy of History". In H. Arendt (ed.), *Illuminations. Essays and Reflections*, tr. H. Zohn. New York: Schocken Books.

Bigo, D. 2007. "Detention of Foreigners, States of Exception and the Social Practices of Control of the Banopticon". In P.K. Rajaram and C. Grundy-Warr (eds.), *Borderscapes. Hidden Geographies and Politics at Territory's Edge*. Minneapolis: University of Minnesota Press.

Clausewitz von, C. 2003. *Vom Kriege*. Erftstadt: Area Verlag.

Foucault, M. 1991. *Discipline and Punish. The Birth of the Prison*, tr. A. Sheridan. London/New York: Penguin Books.

Foucault, M. 1998. *The History of Sexuality. Volume 1. The Will to Knowledge*, tr. R. Hurley. London/New York: Penguin Books.

Foucault, M. 2002. "Confronting Governments: Human Rights". In J.D. Faubion (ed.), *Essential Works of Foucault 1954–1984. Volume 3. Power*, tr. R. Hurley and others. London/New York: Penguin Books.

Lenin, V.I. 2014. *State and Revolution*, tr. T. Chretien. Chicago, IL: Haymarket Books.

Levi, P. 2015. *If this is a man*. In *The Complete Works of Primo Levi*, vol. 1, tr. S. Woolf. New York: Liveright Publishing Corporation.

LGBTQI Refugees GR. 2017. Twitter. 21 May. https://twitter.com/LGBTQIRefugeeGR/status/866328188963737600/photo/1 (Accessed 26 November 2017).

ation, if not exactly and directly of war, at least of the military model as a fundamental means of preventing civil disorder. [...]. If there is a politics-war series that passes through strategy, there is an army-politics series that passes through tactics" (1991: 168).

[2] As Karl Marx was writing to Arnold Ruge, in May 1843, "[...] it is precisely the desperate situation which fills me with hope" (1843).

Malkki, L.H. 1996. "Speechless Emissaries: Refugees, Humanitarianism, and Dehistoricization". *Cultural Anthropology*, 11(3): 377–404. https://doi.org/10.1525/can.1996.11.3.02a00050.

Marx, K. 1843. "Marx to Ruge". https://www.marxists.org/archive/marx/works/1843/letters/43_05.htm (Accessed 16 February 2016).

Marx, K. 1976. *Capital. Vol. I*, tr. B. Fowkes. London/New York: Penguin Books.

Ong, A. 2006. *Neoliberalism as Exception. Mutations in Citizenship and Sovereignty*. Durham/London: Duke University Press.

PART II

Humanist or Capitalist Crisis? Notes and Remarks Concerning a False Dilemma

CHAPTER 7

Exergum

Abstract This chapter is the "Introduction" of Part II of the present book. It is centered on three quotes (by Marx, Lacan and Foucault) that serve as anchor points for the main questions that will be discussed. These quotes are interrelated through three signifiers: *capitalism*, *crisis*, *subject*. A comment on the genealogy and etymology of the signifier "humanism" accompanies them, in order to show the thread that links these signifiers throughout modernity.

Keywords Marx • Lacan • Foucault • Capitalist Crisis • Humanist Crisis • Subject

Let us cite—as an *exergum* or a short introduction—three quotes relating, directly *and* indirectly, with each other and serving as anchor points for the main questions:

> **1.** "The faction of the bourgeoisie that ruled and legislated through the Chambers had a direct interest in the indebtedness of the state. The state deficit was really the main object of its speculation and the chief source of its enrichment. At the end of each year a new deficit. After the lapse of four or five years a new loan. And every new loan offered new opportunities to the finance aristocracy for defrauding the state, which was kept artificially on the verge of bankruptcy—it had to negotiate with the bankers under the most

T. Lagios et al., *Borders, Bodies and Narratives of Crisis in Europe*,
https://doi.org/10.1007/978-3-319-75586-1_7

unfavourable conditions. Each new loan gave a further opportunity, that of plundering the public which invested its capital in state bonds by means of stock-exchange manipulations, the secrets of which the government and the majority in the Chambers were privy to" (Marx 2012: 38–39).

There might be no need for prolix comments regarding the alarming accuracy of the Marxian description of the mechanism of production and distribution of *debt* from the very first steps of capitalism. Every similarity between, on the one hand, the capitalist reality, which emerged at the heart of the "civilised West", in nineteenth-century France, almost 50 years after the outbreak of the French Revolution and the articulation of its ardent slogan "Liberty – Equality – Fraternity", and, on the other hand, the capitalist reality, which emerged at the heart of the EU on the verge of the twenty-first century onwards, almost 50 years after the creation of the European Economic Community, and, at the same time, with the articulation of the EU's ardent motto "*In varietate Concordia*" [*United in diversity*] (EU 2000), is not *coincidental*, a mere product of bad luck or disorder. Contrariwise, this similarity between the historical realities of the nineteenth- and twenty-first-century Europe is a *symptom*, in psychoanalytic terms. If the symptom is a formation through which the existing social order's repressed truth is *re*-inscribed in political terms (Tomŝiç 2015: 6–7), then we should not see this similarity as a simple *disorder*. As Miller claims, "what was holding the symptom together was the saying. The symptom had something to say; it was, definitively, the unconscious intentionality that was holding the symptom together". However, since the increasing use of statistics in the process of diagnosis,[1] "the symptom is henceforth reduced to the trouble. And English says it even better when it speaks of *disorder*, a word that takes its reference from the order of the real" (2004). Thus, if we pay attention to the repressed meaning of this *symptomatic coincidence*, rather than avert our gaze from the historical conjuncture of our present reducing it to a *disorder of reality*, then the EU motto's proclaimed *union* would prove to be a mere saying, while *diversity* would prove to be a real disorder quantified and measured per second in

[1] As Rose pertinently describes, "diagnosis itself has today become a matter of probabilities. It is no longer solely a question of the identification of a condition according to a fixed and categoric taxonomy. Diagnosis itself becomes statistical: a matter of describing a concatenation of indicators, co-occurring in certain regular patterns [...] with a view to developing expert strategies for administering the subjects in a way that minimizes their riskiness" (1996: 21).

the bond yields spreads between Germany and every other Eurozone country, between "centre" and "periphery", according to the hierarchical binary of colonial discourse. If we do not avert our gaze from the historical similarity of the capitalist function, then the repetitive—*in its difference*—function of the mechanism of production and distribution of debt could and should be seen as the *norm,* and not as a *disorder* of our historical, social and political conjuncture; if we do not avert our gaze from the plain fact that the so-called debt crisis was dealt with policies leading to the global debt's growth by climbing more than $70 trillion over the last 10 years to a record high of $215 trillion, according to the Institute of International Finance (Chan 2017), then this historical similarity of the capitalist function could and should be seen as the real crisis, and not as another crisis of the real; it could and should be seen as the real *symptom* of capitalism, and not as a *disorder* of an ideal model of market that could be fixed by its growth. If "commodity fetishism" was the concept that, according to Lacan, reveals that it was Marx and not Freud, the one who invented the notion of "symptom" (Žižek 1989: 18–22) during the phase of "industrial capitalism", then, nowadays, within "financialised capitalism", the *symptom*, namely, the effect of the Symbolic in the Real, is not only "commodity fetishism", but "debt" and "credit" (Lazzarato 2011: 11). If debt as symptom is the saying of the unconscious intentionality of *capitalism*, we should not categorise it as a *dis*order; it might be more fruitful to raise questions regarding its *order*[s]...

> **2.** "You are now, infinitely more than you think, subjects of instruments that, from the microscope right down to the radio-television, are becoming the elements of your existence. You cannot currently even gauge the import of this, but it is nonetheless part of what I am calling scientific discourse, insofar as a discourse is what determines a form of social link" (Lacan 1999: 82).

It is worth noting—besides the groundbreaking and impressively topical character of Lacan's quote—that this, at first sight, exceptionally *anti*-lyrical description of the construction of subjectivity in the technoscientific context of capitalist social reality in contemporary Western societies was included in the *Seminar* that had as its subject the most *lyrical* subject in the West: *Eros* and (corporeal) pleasure. For, 1972–3 *Seminar*'s very title [*Encore*] is heard as *en-corps* [in-body] indicating the inscription of the signifier and of technological gadgets onto history's raw material: the *human body*. As Kittler showed, this is a Nietzschean suggestion to all those who do not remain indifferent towards the relation between inscription and body: "Once the technological differentiation of optics, acoustics, and writing exploded Gutenberg's writing monopoly around 1880, the fabrication of so-called Man became possible. His essence escapes into apparatuses. Machines take over functions of the central nervous system, and no longer, as in times past, merely those of muscles. [...] When it comes to inventing phonography and cinema, the age-old dreams of humankind are no longer sufficient. The physiology of eyes, ears, and brains have to become objects of scientific research. For mechanised writing to be optimised, one can no longer dream of writing as the expression of individuals or the trace of bodies. [...] So-called Man is split up into physiology and information technology" (1999: 16). Charlie Chaplin echoed deafeningly this theoretical insight in *Modern Times* (1936) visualising the co-articulation between *body and machine* in the famous sequence where the "hero" is trapped in the gears of factory machinery (Belton 2013: 65, 175).[2] Thus, Lacan's quote questions not only our narcissistic belief that we are the omnipotent masters of the gadgets we use, but also the naïve belief that technology and its products are beyond good and evil and, eventually, beyond history and its political, social, cultural, and moral determinations; namely, that they depend on the Subject that uses them by the virtue of Reason, while the constantly *updated smart*-phone can be proved *smarter* (brisker) than its user. Surely, nowadays, when even the raw material of human species, DNA, is artificially (re)produced as a storage medium for cultural products,[3] there is no choice or possibility to make time travels into the past and say "no" to technology or science. However, the rejection to fight this rearguard battle does not imply that we should blindly follow what is called "technological progress" without even sparing the time to *question* our technoscientific historical present or attempting to understand the political rationality in which we are histori-

[2] That the body, in the industrialised society, should function as a machine, is evident very clearly in *Modern Times*, as the factory owner watches, through a Panopticon mechanism, even inside the restroom, and appears on a screen ordering the worker to return immediately to work (Potter 2013; Stewart 1976).

[3] "Thanks to an innovative technology for encoding data in DNA strands, two items of world heritage—songs recorded at the Montreux Jazz Festival and digitised by EPFL—have been safeguarded for eternity. This marks the first time that cultural artifacts granted UNESCO heritage status have been saved in such a manner, ensuring they are preserved for thousands of years. The method was developed by US company Twist Bioscience and is being unveiled today in a demonstrator created at the EPFL+ECAL Lab" (Barraud 2017).

cally situated. Heidegger put it in clear terms: "Everywhere we remain unfree and chained to technology, whether we passionately affirm or deny it. But we are delivered over to it in the worst possible way when we regard it as something neutral; for this conception of it, to which today we particularly like to pay homage, makes us utterly blind to the essence of technology" (1993: 312). In equally clear terms, the everyday practice of writing e-mails shows this paradox relation between subject and technology, as the very moment the rational *subject* writes an e-mail, s/he is obliged to put on the top a *subject*, which is essentially the *object* of writing; thusly, the etymological history of the signifier "subject" emerges, albeit unconsciously: "(subjectus: *sub*-under; *jacère*-thrown) denotes the one thrown under, the one who owes fealty to a greater power, be that power language, culture, discourse, history. Over the course of time, the word 'subject' has acquired the status of an *enantioseme*, denoting the sovereignty of the transcendental ego of philosophies of consciousness, whilst retaining the original sense of vassalage, subordination, and so on" (Burke 2008: 102). Which are the consequences of this etymological reinstatement in the everyday practice of the *human subjects* that live, work and speak in technoscientific *capitalism*?

3. "I believe that we should realize that once more the crisis is a sort of theoretical garnish offered by politicians, economists, philosophers and many others, in order to give substance to a present, for which they do not have the tools to analyze. Crisis is, if you will, the permanent present. During the modern history of West, there was never a moment that the deep conscience of a crisis experienced intensely was absent" (Foucault 2001: 1570–2).

Lastly, if Foucault's quote is read not as a provocative—but, in fact, as a modest—description of the current impasse, where politicians, economists, and intellectuals are not in a position to define a way out of the post 2007–8 crisis or—due to its complexity and deep repercussions—even to aptly describe and analyse crisis itself, then we might bear in mind not only the so-called extreme depictions of Western Modernity's impasse—what Lyotard called the "breaking up of the grand Narratives" (1983: 15)—but also the more serene, yet also disquieting, conclusion drawn by Habermas: "modernity can and will no longer borrow the criteria by which it takes its orientation from the models supplied by another epoch; *it has to create its normativity out of itself*" (1998: 7). Due to the breaking up of the grand Narrative that free-market economy could create its normativity out of itself, as the 2007–8 crisis of financialised capitalism proved to be "a diagnostic error", because "far from impairing neo-liberal policies, the crisis led to their dramatic *reinforcement*" (Dardot and Laval 2013: 1), the question concerning normativity and the lack of our theoretical tools to analyse crisis and our present has (re)emerged. What is called nowadays "information society" emerged through a series of modern revolutions: Copernican Revolution, Scientific Revolution and Industrial Revolution. Modernity became the synonym of Revolutionary, since to be in modernity means to have the desire to leave the past and the tradition behind and to revolutionise the present through constant innovations and mutations; in a word, through permanent "modernisation". As Rimbaud summarised it in a really modern categorical imperative: "*Il faut être absolument moderne*" [*One must be absolutely modern*] (2008: 243). Of course, this imperative had the analogous consequences aptly articulated on 13 May 1871: "*Je* est un *autre*" [*I* is an *other*] (ibid: 113). Namely, *modernity* is also the synonym of *crisis*. Nevertheless, Foucault's quote suggests something more; not only that modernity is a historical series of crises, but also—due to the lack of theoretical tools—that modernity is the crisis of *crisis*, namely, the crisis of *critique*.[4] If, according to Foucault, crisis is the permanent present that politicians, economists, philosophers and many others cannot analyse, then it comes as no surprise that he returned to questions articulated in a Kantian form relating to our present: *What is Enlightenment*? (Foucault 2000). Or, through a slight displacement of the signifier, as modernity and crisis are synonyms: *What is Critique*? (Foucault 1997). Nonetheless, this Kantian *form* of questions should not obscure the Nietzschean *content* of the critique to the traditional concept of "humanism". As Foucault suggested, "we must not conclude that everything which has ever been linked with humanism is to be rejected, but that the humanistic thematic is in itself too supple, too diverse, too inconsistent to serve as an axis for reflection. And it is a fact that, at least since the seventeenth century, what is called 'humanism' has always been obliged to lean on certain conceptions of man borrowed from religion, science, or politics. [...] From this

[4] The etymology shows the common root of *crisis* and *critique* and is rather enlightening for the fact that critique has as its presupposition a crisis: crisis (n.) early 15c., from Latinised form of Greek *krisis* "turning point in a disease" (used as such by Hippocrates and Galen), literally "judgment, result of a trial, selection", from *krinein* "to separate, decide, judge", from PIE root *krei- "to sieve", thus "discriminate, distinguish". Transferred non-medical sense is 1620s in English (Online Etymology Dictionary: "Crisis").

standpoint, I am inclined to see Enlightenment and humanism in a state of tension rather than identity" (2000: 314). Foucault's historicalisation of modernity raises a crucial question: which exactly is the relation between modernity and humanism?

Consequently, we could discern that these three quotes are related directly *and* indirectly, because there is a chain of three signifiers that connects them explicitly *or* implicitly: *capitalism, subject, crisis.* But where is this chain of signifiers anchored? Where exactly this signifying chain, by which Marx, Lacan and Foucault describe their present and detect the interrelation between *capitalism, subject* and *crisis,* is, in Lacanian terms, anchored or quilted (Evans 1996: 149; Dor 1998: 32)? Where exactly, on which sign, are these signifiers knotted together with a signified (Lacan 1997: 259–270)? In our view, this anchoring point, where these signifiers are knotted together, is "humanism".

Since "the meaning of 'humanism' has so many shades that to analyse all of them is hardly feasible", as it can fluctuate even in the same language (Giustiniani 1985: 167), it would be more useful to emphasise that "humanism" is a word with a very recent history; in fact, a very modern one, which overlaps modernity itself, as the signifier did not appear before the sixteenth century, but its signified was then very narrow, referring only "to a student of ancient languages or more widely to sophisticated academics of any subjects other than theology" (Corpson and Grayling 2015: 1–2). More importantly, the most prevalent of its current signifieds, referring to "those who proposed in one way or another to alleviate human suffering in general and/or advance the human race in general" (Calhoun 2008: 77), emerged only *after* the Industrial Revolution and the establishment of capitalism in the early nineteenth century. It was only then that "humanism" in its modern sense was invented (Davies 1997: 7–34). And this invention, despite that its very form was "doomed to be a perpetual *signum contradictionis*" (Giustiniani 1985: 195), began to be globalised in full accordance with the historical, social and political matrix that produced it. It really seems that a sign like "humanism", with a history of signification full of contradictions, was necessary for the transcendence of capitalism's internal contradictions and crises.

For, at the time capitalism had its first crises during the process to modernise the whole world, the latter was met with the first "humanitarian crisis" and the first wave of globalisation, that is, the process of creating the world in the image of the dominant class (Marx and Engels 2012: 40), that is, with another wave of the tsunami known as "colonialism" (Cooper

2005: 104). The projects of humanism's advocates were projects of advancing the human and "closely related to the ideas of civilization, modernization, and, eventually, evolution. France's *mission civilisatrice* was understood as humanitarian, bringing civilization to those suffering from the lack of being French or even European. Colonialism itself was often understood (with no cynicism) as humanitarian. Christian missionaries (working largely within the context of colonialism) pursued humanitarian missions" (Calhoun 2008: 77–8). The French "civilising mission" was not an absolutely national phenomenon, but a Western one, as its inscription onto language shows; for, the French verb "humanizer" has as its meaning the same one that the English borrowed in order to express the capitalist reality of human beings globally: "Make (something) more humane or civilized" (Oxford English Dictionary: "humanize"). Here, we should notice that the sign between brackets in the definition above clearly shows that the human *subject* is also an *object* in the humanisation process.

On the one hand, this *subject-object* relation was clearly depicted by Fanon at the *outside* of the West, as the interrelation between humanism and colonialism under the pretext of modernisation and civilisation: "Europe undertook the leadership of the world with ardour, cynicism and violence. […] That same Europe where they were never done talking of Man, and where they never stopped proclaiming that they were only anxious for the welfare of Man: today we know with what sufferings humanity has paid for every one of their triumphs of the mind" (1963: 163; also, Young 1990; Pennycook 1998). On the other hand, Foucault depicted the historical reality of this relation at the *inside* of the West, where "Western Man" became *subjected* to a nexus of power-knowledge relations that constructs his/her (self-)consciousness through its inscription onto the human body, as the interrelation between humanism and modernisation under the pretext of autonomy and liberty shows: "It would be wrong to say that the soul is an illusion, or an ideological effect. On the contrary, it exists, it has a reality, it is produced permanently around, on, within the body by the functioning of a power that is exercised on those punished – and, in a more general way, on those one supervises, trains and corrects, over madmen, children at home and at school, the colonized, over those who are stuck at a machine and supervised for the rest of their lives. […] The man described for us, whom we are invited to free, is already in himself the effect of a subjection much more profound than himself. A 'soul' inhabits him and brings him to existence, which is itself a factor in the mastery that power exercises over the body. The soul is the effect and instrument of a political anatomy; the soul is the prison of the body" (1991: 29–30). Consequently, the "historical *a priori*" of the modern political economy of the *capital* was the modern political anatomy of the *body*; the term "human resources" is eloquent enough for this historical bond.

Therefore, a series of questions arises: is there a capitalist crisis that is not *always already*, namely, *in principle* and *by definition*, a humanist crisis? And vice versa: is there a humanist crisis that is not *always already*, namely, *in principle* and *by definition*, a capitalist one? And more crucially: how could it be an actual need for *critical* thinking, if there is not a crisis that pre-exists and embraces both the social reality and the subjectivities constituted within it? Therefore: is there a capitalist crisis that does not constitute and does not establish fundamentally and thoroughly the human subjectivity and, conversely, is there a human subjectivity that remains safe and sound during a capitalist crisis? Or rather: how could we understand the signifier "Crisis", without even thinking about the *historical connection*, that is the social, political, economic, scientific and cultural construction of the signifiers "capitalism" and "human" during modernity, namely, as Althusser has warned us (2010: 233), without even paying attention to their *unconscious chaining*?

References

Althusser, L. 2010. *For Marx*, tr. B. Brewster. London/New York: Verso.

Barraud, E. 2017. "Two Items of Music Anthology Now Stored for Eternity in DNA". https://phys.org/news/2017-09-items-music-anthology-eternity-dna.html#jCp (Accessed 30 September 2017).

Belton, J. 2013. *American Cinema, American Culture*. New York: McGraw Hill.

Burke, S. 2008. *The Death and Return of the Author. Criticism and Subjectivity in Barthes, Foucault, and Derrida*. Edinburgh: Edinburgh University Press.

Calhoun, C. 2008. "The Imperative to Reduce Suffering". In M. Barnett and T. G. Weiss (eds.), *Humanitarianism in Question: Politics, Power, Ethics*. New York/London: Cornell University Press.

Chan, S.P. 2017. "Global Debt Explodes at 'Eye-watering' Pace to Hit £170 Trillion". http://www.telegraph.co.uk/business/2017/04/04/global-debt-explodes-eye-watering-pace-hit-170-trillion/ (Accessed 29 September 2017).

Corpson, A. and Grayling, A.C. 2015. *The Wiley Blackwell Handbook of Humanism*. Oxford: Wiley Blackwell.

Cooper, F. 2005. *Colonialism in Question. Theory, Knowledge, History*. London/Berkeley: University of California Press.

Davies, T. 1997. *Humanism*. London/New York: Routledge.

Dardot, P. and Laval, C. 2013. *The New Way of the World: On Neoliberal Society*, tr. G. Elliot. London/New York: Verso.
Dor, J. 1998. *Introduction to the Reading of Lacan: The Unconscious Structured Like a Language*, tr. S. Fairfield. New York: Other Press.
EU. 2000. *Motto*. https://europa.eu/european-union/about-eu/symbols/motto_en (Accessed 15 September 2017).
Evans, D. 1996. *An Introductory Dictionary of Lacanian Psychoanalysis*. London: Routledge.
Fanon, F. 1963. *The Wretched of the Earth*, tr. C. Farrington. Harmondsworth: Penguin.
Foucault, M. 1991. *Discipline and Punish*, tr. A. Sheridan. London/New York: Penguin.
Foucault, M. 1997. "What is Critique?". In M. Foucault, *The Politics of Truth*. Los Angeles: Semiotext(e).
Foucault, M. 2000. "What is Enlightenment". In M. Foucault, *Essential Works of Foucault 1954–1984, vol. 1, Ethics*, tr. R. Hurley & Others. London/New York: Penguin.
Foucault, M. 2001. "La politique est la continuation de la guerre par d' autres moyens". In M. Foucault, *Dits et écrits, I, 1954–1975*. Paris: Quarto Gallimard.
Giustiniani, V.R. 1985. "Homo, Humanus, and the Meanings of 'Humanism'". *Journal of the History of Ideas*, 46(2): 167–195.
Habermas, J. 1998. *The Philosophical Discourse of Modernity*, tr. F. Lawrence. Cambridge: Polity Press.
Heidegger, M. 1993. "The Question concerning Technology". In M. Heidegger, *Basic Writings*. San Francisco: Harper.
Kittler, F. 1999. *Gramophone, Film, Typewriter*, tr. G. Winthrop-Young and M. Wutz. Stanford: Stanford University Press.
Lacan, J. 1997. *Seminar III, 1955–56, The Psychoses*, tr. R. Grigg. New York/London: W.W. Norton & Company.
Lacan, J. 1999. *Seminar XX, 1972–73, Encore*, tr. B. Fink. New York/London: W.W. Norton & Company.
Lazzarato, M. 2011. *The Making of the Indebted Man, An Essay on the Neoliberal Condition*, tr. J. D. Jordan. Amsterdam: Semiotext(e).
Lyotard, J.-F. 1983. *The Postmodern Condition*, tr. G. Bennington, B. Massumi. Minneapolis: University of Minnesota Press.
Marx, K. 2012. *The Class Struggles in France, 1848 to 1850*. Chicago: Aristeus Books.
Marx, K. & Engels, F. 2012. *The Communist Manifesto: A modern edition*. London: Verso.
Miller, J.A. 2004. "A Fantasy". http://2012.congresoamp.com/en/template.php?file=Textos/Conferencia-de-Jacques-Alain-Miller-en-Comandatuba.html (Accessed 2 April 2016).

Online Etymology Dictionary. "Crisis". https://www.etymonline.com/word/crisis (Accessed 25 June 2017).

Oxford English Dictionary. "Humanize". https://en.oxforddictionaries.com/definition/humanize (Accessed 20 June 2017).

Pennycook, A. 1998. *English and the Discourses of Colonialism*. London/New York: Routledge.

Potter, G. 2013. "The Tramp & the Culture Industry: Adorno, Chaplin, and the Possibility of Progressive Comedy". *Arizona Quarterly: A Journal of American Literature, Culture, and Theory*, 69(1): 73–90. https://doi.org/10.1353/arq.2013.0002.

Rimbaud, A. 2008. *Complete Works*, tr. P. Schmidt. New York/London: HarperCollins.

Rose, N. 1996. "Psychiatry as a Political Science: Advanced Liberalism and the Administration of Risk". *History of the Human Sciences*. 9(2): 1–23.

Stewart, G. 1976. "Modern Hard Times: Chaplin and the Cinema of Self-Reflection". *Critical Inquiry*, 3(2): 295–314.

Tomšiç, S. 2015. *The Capitalist Unconscious: Marx and Lacan*. London/New York: Verso.

Young, R. 1990. *White Mythologies: Writing history and the West*. London: Routledge.

Žižek, S. 1989. *The Sublime Object of Ideology*. London/New York: Verso.

CHAPTER 8

Discourses on Crisis and Critical Discourse

Abstract In this chapter, the discussion revolves around the discourses about the 2007–8 financial crisis and the paradoxical interpretations that were circulated in the ranks of both dominant and critical discourse. The paradox lies in the fact that, while the crisis was initially interpreted as a "capitalist" one, very soon a displacement of the signifiers took place, and its interpretation as "humanist" became the dominant one. This displacement is based on a repression and oblivion of capitalist function and its historical link with modern subjectivity.

Keywords Marx • Nietzsche • Foucault • Lacan • Capital Controls • Credit

All the political powers and all the economists—whether belonging to the so-called progressive camp or not—concord and proclaim that we live in a period of "crisis" with worldwide consequences. After all, everyone knows that when the US president begins his speech to the US people by saying "Good evening. This is an extraordinary period for America's economy" (Bush 2008), the signifiers "extraordinary period" imply serious consequences for the whole world. However, when he adds that, although he believes in free-market principles, he is obliged to act against them, since "companies that make bad decisions should be allowed to go out of business. Under normal circumstances, I would have followed this course. But

T. Lagios et al., *Borders, Bodies and Narratives of Crisis in Europe*,
https://doi.org/10.1007/978-3-319-75586-1_8

these are not normal circumstances", some crucial questions arise. What has caused these depictions by Bush, articulated in Foucauldian and Agambenian terms, such as *abnormal* situation of a *state of exception*? Why was Bush obligated not to follow the course he believed in, but the exact opposite? Bush's claims that "our 21st-century global economy remains regulated largely by outdated 20th-century laws" and that "democratic capitalism is the best system ever devised" should be heard as an attempt to thread the needle; thus, they became the basis for criticisms that US Government's response to crisis created a "growing sense of schizophrenia", since "much of the public debate has centered on the role of government in the markets precisely because it became so involved *after* refusing to do whatever it took to save Lehman" (Williams 2010: 212). As Shakespeare remarked about a paradoxical sequence of actions concerning another abnormal situation in another state of exception, "time is out of joint" (2005: *Hamlet*, I.5).

However, one should wonder if, eventually, the aforementioned "sense of schizophrenia" is produced by a discourse that, on the one hand, criticises Bush, while admitting that "risk in investment banking is *as natural as air*– without it, investment banks can't breathe", while, on the other hand, it describes people taking decisions about risk as "gamblers", whose "profits from winning bets must outweigh the losses; if not, the gambler is out of business" (Williams 2010: 105; emphasis added). Namely, one should wonder if, eventually, the "sense of schizophrenia" is produced, when, in order not to underutilise *capital*, human subjects are told that they *are free to gamble and take risks*; but, *at the same time*, in order to avoid capital loss, human *subjects* are told that they *should be subjected to* the "extensive modeling used to measure risk taking", and not submit to the "dangerous *sentiment* that views risk management as a constraint to the profit" (ibid; emphasis added). As Marx demonstrated, the sentiment that views risk management as a constraint to the profit is *schizophrenic* or *dangerous* in terms of *morals*, but it is considered absolutely consonant with the inherent *logic and rationality* of capitalist *economy*, because capital should be always in circulation and never in inertia. In Harvey's words, "capital is not a thing, but rather a process that exists only in motion. When circulation stops, value disappears and the whole system comes tumbling down" (2010: 12). Thus, if capital is not a thing, but a process in constant *motion*, then capital could be seen primarily as a *play*, meaning etymologically the "free or unimpeded movement" of mechanisms, and so on.[1] For, in order not to underutilise *capital* in the financial sphere, human *subjects* should be subjected to the process of *gambling*, while, at the same time, they consider this subjection "as natural as air". Or, as Huizinga showed in 1949, at the moment where industrial capitalism was moving to its post-war financialisation, "pure avarice neither trades nor plays; it does not gamble. To dare, to take risks, to bear uncertainty, to endure tension-these are the essence of the play spirit. Tension adds to the importance of the game and, as it increases, enables the player to forget that he is only playing" (1949: 58). Consequently, it could be said that expecting from a gambler to be responsible or to act without risk and uncertainty is politically schizophrenic and a dangerous sentimentalism. As etymology shows, this expectation is a *contradiction in terms*, since "play" and "responsibility" are in direct opposition and conflict. This contradiction in terms was inscribed onto another term that has been used (Williams 2010: 218), in order to describe the causes for the financial crisis: "moral hazard". This term understood by economists to describe loss-increasing behaviour that arises under insurance, by having a strong rhetorical tone, bears a normative judgement with theological connotations, since it recognises unquestioningly an archetypal "reasonable man" and also implicitly the existence of the "unreasonable man" (Rowell and Connelly 2012); consequently, it simply reproduces the "sense of schizophrenia" without explaining its very *conditions of possibility*.

Therefore, it should come as no surprise that, as the crisis was deepening and expanding throughout the world threatening the global financial and banking system with collapse, a paradox appeared: the interpretation of the "humanist crisis" began to emerge as the dominant one, not only by the so-called (neo)liberals, but even in the ranks of those who were willing to denounce or criticise the established political, social and economic order. For example, in the USA, leading economists who were willing to criticise Bush's government and the neoliberal function of the

[1] Etymology shows the common thread between the signifiers "play", "game" and "gamble". While "play" is the *unimpeded* movement, "game" shows the fun and the amusement produced by this *unimpeded* movement. "Gamble" until the eighteenth century means "play games" (see, Online Etymology Dictionary: "play", "game", "gamble"). Moreover, this etymological relation between "play" and "game" reemerged convolutedly during the last century, as "French mathematicians rendered *game* as *jeu* and created a heterolinguistic supersign *jeu*/game in the course of introducing John von Neumann and Oskar Morgenstern's mathematical theory of games applicable to economics and nuclear warfare" (Liu 2010).

market, such as Batra, Roubini and Stiglitz, remained confined to a moral critique, which reproduced and resurrected the discursive regime of the debate between Keynes and Hayek, failing to historicise the current crisis and, consequently, leaving intact the present structure of power, knowledge and economy that produces a bio-political calculative rationality (Hanan and Chaput 2013). In Europe, instead of deepening and expanding the critique to the capitalist function, which resulted in the deeper and greater crisis since the 1929 crash, there was a displacement towards the abstract appeal to humanist ideals or to an idealised European past. The political elites did not hasten to respond to the voices that, after 2007–8, were talking about a capitalist crisis: in 2009, in Paris at the opening of the economic symposium "New World, New Capitalism", the French president Sarkozy offered a mixture of critique on financial capitalism under the perspective of humanist values, as, in his view, "financial capitalism is a system of irresponsibility and ... is amoral. It is a system where the logic of the market excuses everything". Sarkozy's *moral* critique was supported by Merkel and Blair who called for more supervision of the markets by politics (*DW* Staff 2009). In Greece, the displacement from "capitalist" to "humanist" crisis emerged clearly in SYRIZA's rhetoric since 2012 and was plainly evident into the "Thessaloniki Manifesto" (2014), where the austerity measures were described as the cause of a "humanitarian crisis" in Greece, and not as the result of a global capitalist crisis (Katsourides 2016; Mudde 2017), neither as the metonymy of the capitalist restructuring of the Greek economy. Nevertheless, a brief look at Europe's history would suffice to inform all the aforementioned leaders that humanism in capitalist Europe has *always already* been at a crisis, at the same time with the establishment and the expansion of the capitalist function, at least 160 years before the Greek debt crisis.[2]

In this context, it is rather difficult not to see how Nietzsche's infamous aphorism is really timely and crucial for the understanding of our historical conjuncture: "Against positivism, which halts at phenomena – 'There are only facts' – I would say: No, facts is precisely what there is not, only

[2] As the German poet Joseph von Eichendorff lamented in a letter in August 1849, namely, after the defeat of the 1848 revolutionary movements that swept Europe and just before the great capitalist growth, humanism and its values were already in deep crisis, at least since Shakespeare's age: "Truly, if I were younger and wealthier than I unfortunately am, I'd emigrate to America today. Not out of cowardice – for the times can do me personally as little harm as I can do them – but out of over-powering disgust at the moral rottenness which, to use Shakespeare's phrase, stinks to high heaven" (cited in Hobsbawm 1995: 21).

interpretations" (1968: §481). For, in the course of time, although the signifier "crisis" remained at the forefront, the signifier "capitalist" or "financial" was repressed, in psychoanalytic terms, that is, it has been falling—gradually, but steadily—into oblivion. Its place was taken, as politics and its rhetoric abhor vacuum, by the signifier "humanist", since the consequences of the austerity measures and fiscal adjustment began to materialise at the expense of the lower social classes and since the flows of migrants began to substitute the flows of capital not only in Greece, but all over Europe. It is really evident that at the peak of the so-called negotiations between Greek government and Troika the emphasis of SYRIZA's rhetoric was put on the social-democratic interpretation of "humanitarian crisis" (Katsourides 2016: 101–5). Moreover, the infamous Schäuble's plan for a five-year Grexit included a package of "humanitarian aid" to mitigate acute emergencies, as if these emergencies would be caused from a *"natural" disaster* and not from a *political decision.*

Accordingly, the signifying chain regarding crisis was broken and restored by the dominant discourse, leaving the critical discourse almost speechless in front of a false dilemma between capitalist or humanist crisis, on the one side, and an undisputable fact that there is a crisis that haunts Western societies, on the other. If we paraphrase *Communist Manifesto*'s opening (Marx and Engels 2012: 33), "a spectre is haunting Europe – the spectre of Crisis. All the Powers of old Europe have entered into a holy alliance to exorcise this spectre: Merkel and Hollande, believers and atheists, French social-democrats and German conservatives". To be sure, the crisis was initially interpreted as a "crisis of financial capitalism", since its tangible starting point was Lehman Brothers' file for Chapter 11 bankruptcy protection on 15 September 2008, the largest bankruptcy filing in US history, due to the crisis at the US subprime mortgage market that began a year earlier. However, this very fact haunting our present needs to be seen as an interpretation itself, and not as a fact that is beyond interpretation, like a *spectre*; consequently, it should be interpreted with the appropriate theoretical tools, as Foucault remarked. In Greece, for example, all the political powers—from the neo-Nazi party Golden Dawn to the leftists and anarchists—agree and recognise the fact that we live in a "crisis"; however, their inability and reluctance to address the crucial questions regarding crisis are so deep that, while a century ago, the Leninist question "what is to be done?"[3] was a necessary and sufficient condition to form a

[3] In fact, the question "What is to be done?" had been articulated in 1863 by Nikolai Chernyshevsky, a Russian radical journalist and scholar, whose novel *What is to be done?* was

revolutionary vanguard, nowadays the only question that is addressed in agony and anxiety for society's future is "what is going to happen?". This perplexity and bewilderment is clear evidence that the monotonous repetition and invocation of the signifier "crisis", instead of its historicalisation, is not a necessary and sufficient condition to comprehend the phenomenon, on the one hand, and to categorise anyone in the ranks of critique, on the other. We should not cast to oblivion the fact that in view of the Greek referendum (5 July 2015) about the Greek government's position towards the Troika's proposal for agreement, both opponent camps, the supporters of "Yes", as well as the supporters of "No", based their argumentation almost exclusively on the signifier "crisis"; the former were deeply convinced that, due to the crisis, a docile policy towards debtors should be imposed, as *There Is No Alternative*, while the latter were deeply convinced that due to the crisis the solution was the disobedience to Troika and the rejection of the bailout conditions, since the continuous austerity was catastrophic. Thus, there should have been no surprise that, before the dawn of 6 July 2015, a slippage of signifiers took place, as the Greek people had said "No" (61.31%) to the bailout conditions, while the Greek government said a "Yes" to a more painful agreement proposed by the debtors, confirming Nietzsche's suspicion concerning the relation between facts and interpretation.

This suspicion cannot be suspended or confuted through the promotion of an intersubjective communication or democratic consensus *à la* Habermas (Fultner 2014), because these concepts have been already proved to be pretexts for the stability and seamless function of the established order in the late capitalist context. The facts are quite eloquent: almost all of the issues under discussion in the so-called negotiations between the debtors and the creditors after the EU "debt crisis" had *already* been the subject of a dialogue that took place in 1989 in Washington; this dialogue included those participants that were interested in forming a consensus, namely IMF, World Bank and the US Treasury, and excluded all those that were going to be the *subjects* of the aforementioned consensus. This consensus between these three Washington-based institutions was called the "Washington Consensus" and had three main targets: a market economy, openness to the world and macroeconomic discipline as a response to the end of industrial-based economy and the

Lenin's favourite. Lenin was carrying always with him a photo of Chernyshevsky, as well as photos of Marx, Engels, Herzen and Pisarev (Lih 2008, 2011).

leading role of the State (Serra and Stiglitz 2008: 3). These facts could be faced either with Marcellus fear in the view of the spectre of Hamlet's father, a fear that is sufficient to remark that "something is rotten in the state of Denmark" criticising thusly the moral and political corruption (Shakespeare 2005: *Hamlet*, I.4), or with the required suspicion towards the signifiers that are supposed to foster unmediated reflection—beyond any interpretation—of the mere facts in and from themselves, according to the doctrine of ***adaequatio***, namely, the adequate relation between words and things, as it was formulated from Plato to Habermas and Chomsky (Leclerc 2006).

For, only by being suspicious towards the dominant discourse on crisis, one could discern that contemporary discourse, whether critical or not, performs, consciously or not, a constant slippage from the signifier "capitalist" to "humanist", in order to denote and signify the quasi *Master Signifier* (to use a Lacanian term) that dominates, that is, "crisis". As this false dilemma regarding the nature and the character of the crisis is discursively constructed, a paradox is emerging, since not only the critical discourse, but also the dominant one, tends to use the signifier "crisis", agreeing that there is a crisis and disagreeing only about its nature and its character, while the slippage from the signifier "capitalist" to the "humanist" is repressed and becomes unnoticed, even though everyone asserts that the catalyst for the eruption of the crisis was financial by definition. In order not only to understand the presuppositions and consequences of this paradoxical false dilemma and the logic of its signifiers, but also to remain suspicious about the relation between facts and interpretation, a critical discourse should put emphasis on, and pay attention to, the radicality of the Lacanian undertaking to transcribe his position "the unconscious is structured like language" to that of "the unconscious is politics", as Miller remarked (2002). This transcription is crucial for the understanding of the logic of the signifier, on which contemporary relations between unconscious and politics, between facts and interpretation, are based. While Freud maintained that "politics is the unconscious", Lacan reversed and displaced this thesis. Under the guise of continuity between these two enunciations, "an unexpected inversion is produced, as politics seems to be occupying, contaminating even, the unconscious itself, the sole domain that is within the competence of psychoanalysis. With this intrusion of politics into the unconscious, the very subject-matter of psychoanalysis, something is surreptitiously added that suspends, ruins even, the classic, Freudian thesis: 'politics is the unconscious'. What this thesis [Lacan's], according to which the unconscious dominates politics, immediately implies is that the social bond at stake in politics is governed by a certain logic that operates unbeknown to men thus brought together, a logic that 'is already operative in the unconscious', namely the logic of the signifier" (Šumiç 2016: 28–29). This unbeknown logic of the signifier traverses the relation between politics and unconscious and by being already operative in the unconscious creates a paradox, which is easily observed, but it cannot be explained or resolved by a "discourse analysis" that does not focus on the *historicity* and the genealogical emergence of the various rules allowing the emergence of the signifier and its slippage. This logic of the signifier results, on the one hand, in the unanimous moral condemnation of crisis and, on the other, in a disagreement only about the two adjectives that should characterise and depict it, while, simultaneously, the latter replaces steadily the former: *capitalist* or *humanist*?

Consequently, it is absolutely crucial to raise questions about the *material* presupposition, or rather, *historical* condition of possibility, for the opportunity given to Greek people to express their opinion in a referendum; namely, to raise questions about the "capital controls", because without the imposition of "capital controls" on the Greek banks, the announcement of the referendum would inevitably cause a "bank run", since during the week before the announcement of the referendum, 1.3 billion euros were withdrawn from the Greek banking system due to the lack of agreement between Greece and Troika (Anderson 2015). At this point, a question emerges showing that historical time was literally "out of joint". For, how can one maintain that capital controls were the *material* presupposition of the referendum, since capital controls were imposed right *after* the announcement of the referendum? In order to answer this reasonable question, it might be useful to raise some questions of a different rationality: what if the signifier that is read as *noun* ("controls") should, in fact, be read and interpreted as *verb*? What if we make an attempt to interpret the fact of capital controls by subverting its syntax and its grammatical order, namely, if we avoid to read the signifiers "capital controls" as a combination of *adjective + noun*, but in a form of *subject + verb*? What if we—following the most infamous philologist's advice that "the seigneurial privilege of giving names even allows us to conceive of the origin of language itself as a manifestation of the power of the rulers: they say 'this *is* so and so', they set their seal on everything and every occurrence with a sound and thereby take possession of it, as it were" (Nietzsche 2006: I, §2)—make a move from the level of grammatical order of *signs* to that of political syntax of *powers*, in order to see the power of the order and the order of the power to be fully manifested through the logic of the signifiers that relates unconscious and politics?

That move shows that—even within the context of what is called "democratic capitalism"—it is the Capital that *controls* society, and not the (Greek) government; it shows that the *subject* that controls the capital flows is not the elected representative of the (Greek) society, but there is a self-referential order of powers: capital *controls* capital as a financial relation that transverses the social and political field. That move shows that the referendum could not be held, that the opportunity to ask Greek people would be impossible to take place without the control of the Capital. That move shows that nearly a decade after the outbreak of the 2007–8 crisis, capitalism and its dominant *ideology*, which wholesale is called "neoliberalism", instead of being—or even when they give the impression that they are being "in retreat"—they gain ground in the field of social practices (Crouch 2011). For, the current crisis emerged in a globalised capitalist system, where as Lazzarato aptly summarises "the creditor-debtor relation concerns the entirety of the current population as well as the population to come. Economists tell us that every French child is born 22,000 euros in debt. We are no longer the inheritors of original sin but rather of the debt of preceding generations. 'Indebted man' is subject to a creditor-debtor power relation accompanying him throughout his life, from birth to death. If in times past we were indebted to the community, to the gods, to our ancestors, we are henceforth indebted to the 'god' Capital" (2011: 32). Or as Žižek described at the end of the Cold War, "it is as if the retreat of the Master in capitalism was only a displacement: as if the defetishization in the 'relations between men' was paid for by the emergence of fetishism in the 'relations between things' – by commodity fetishism" (Žižek 1989: 22). Therefore, we could say that if the feudal serf being *unfree* trembled lest his/her body being whipped by the feudal lord, today the consumer, either being employed or unemployed in the *free* market, is trembling lest his/her creditworthiness is rated lowly; if previously the criminal's skin was *marked* permanently as a stigma for the offence representing the seal of the Law, now the seal of the Law and Order *marks* permanently his/her cheque books and credit cards; if in the past a part of the debtor's body was *maimed*, now his/her deposits run the risk of a "hair-*cut*". Consequently, a discourse that remains only a humanist critique of this situation tends to ignore its social, political and scientific-technological aspects or a discourse that remains merely a critique of capitalist economy tends to overlook the deep relation between a capitalist restructure of the social, political and economic field and the constitution and construction of the subjectivities in the historical conjuncture called "neoliberalism". As Dardot and Laval suggest, "[n]eo-liberalism is not merely destructive of rules, institutions and rights. It is also *productive* of certain kinds of social relations, certain ways of living, certain subjectivities. In other words, at stake in neo-liberalism is nothing more, nor less, than the *form of our existence* – the way in which we are led to conduct ourselves, to relate to others and to ourselves. Neo-liberalism defines a certain existential norm in western societies and, far beyond them, in all those societies that follow them on the path of 'modernity'" (2013: 3).

Thus, while the referendum's result was a *stentorian* "No" to what was seen as a *debtor's* ultimatum, a signifiers' displacement took place and "No" became a "Yes" without the slightest protest. Admittedly, the reasons for this displacement and its passive acceptance are manifold. However, we should pay attention to the fact that *after* the imposition of capital controls, a cash-oriented population was *silently*, massively and overnight led to conduct itself digitally and was *silently* subjected to the strategy of those who voted "Yes" in daily practice and supported "Yes" as "a form of existence": the numbers of *debit* cards issued only in the month of the referendum (July 2015) surpassed that of the whole previous year. Only the National Bank of Greece issued 400,000 debit cards in four weeks (*The Telegraph* 2015; *Euromonitor* 2017). Thus, Greek people voted "No" to their debtors, while, at the same time their everyday practice, their *habitus*,[4] in Bourdieu's terms, had *already* begun to be radically transformed resulting in their digital *subjection* to the banking system. This very fact could be seen as the interpretation of the disjointedness of time, namely of the fact that on 27 June 2015 the referendum was announced and *after* one day the capital controls were imposed, even though the former could not have taken place without the latter. This could be seen as the moment when the payment infrastructure turned political (Bátiz-Lazo et al. 2015), when the ATMs became the field of political conflict substituting the ballot boxes. However, this conflict was

[4] As it has been aptly remarked, "Bourdieu summarizes this relation using the following equation: [(habitus)(capital)] + field = practice. This equation can be unpacked as stating: practice results from relations between one's dispositions (habitus) and one's position in a field (capital), within the current state of play of that social arena (field)" (Maton 2008: 51).

easily pacified and almost entirely overlooked, since "in critical economic situations, where a bank run, bank insolvency, or bail-in are likely to happen, the role of ATMs becomes technocratic, securing peace through controlled circulation of money and transactions with restrictions". This was apparent in Cyprus, where "apart from some small-scale demonstrations, no major riots were recorded. In this, we detect a direct, decisive connection between ATMs, civil obedience and political preservation" (Efthymiou and Michael 2015: 134). In Greece, there was an attempt to make ATMs sites of resistance, as protesters destroyed many or overwhelmed them with graffiti and stickers, inviting people to demonstrate against a third memorandum and resist ATM withdrawals. Nevertheless, due to the inability of critical discourse to realise neoliberalism's transformative power of everyday practice and its technoscientific means of change, the ballot box was still seen by the vast majority as a more appropriate site for resistance hoping that no transaction error could appear there.

Yet, as Deleuze claimed, contemporary societies of control are based on a *numerical language* with floating signifiers representing currencies and financial flows, and not on a *grammatical order* with alphabetical hierarchy representing the connection between currencies and a gold standard. Thus, the *control* of the capital flows has been coupled with the *discipline* of the population (Deleuze 1992). Control and discipline have been combined in the digital era, resulting in a new and different, namely, modern, all-too modern triangular form of *sovereignty*, *discipline* and *governmentality* through control on the pretext of security, as Foucault demonstrated (2007: 107–8). If the critical discourse in Greece could be historically suspicious and critical of the established logic of the signifiers, it might have taken into consideration the fact that Capital *controls* contemporary societies by controlling and disciplining the form of everyday existence and practice.[5] If Capital *controls* contemporary societies, then the

[5] Admittedly, Deleuze and Foucault were not prophets. They had *already* witnessed this transformation in France after May '68 and the consequent decline of critique. For, neither political violence nor elections have been effective in subverting or obstructing bio-political control, as Capital had *already* started taking measures against its critics, in order to *control* and *discipline* individual and social body. Historical details: the first ATM had *already* been in function before May and at another place, as Barclay's materialised the 24/7 capitalism on 27 June 1967 at London (Robat 2006). In France, the 1966–1967 "Debré reformations" paved the way for the invasion of banks into the households: in 1968, ATM cards are introduced; in 1969, only 10% of salaries are paid monthly via personal bank accounts, while 75% in 1972 (de Blic and Lazarus 2007: 51–63). Bourdieu describes this process as "democrati-

disjointedness of time cannot be repaired by any "old mole", as Hegel and Marx hoped following a teleological linear time like Hamlet (Derrida 1994; de Grazia 1999). If Capital *controls* contemporary societies, then the disjointedness of time is the way that modern history appears, because Capital is doomed in *repetition* to modernise, since "what Marx grasped in *Capital* is the repetition compulsion inherent in capital's movement towards accumulation. Capital is driven to self-reproduction through a ceaseless process of differentiation, and this process is unable to avoid the repetitive business cycle of recession, prosperity, economic crisis, recession" (Karatani 2012: 1).

Consequently, there might be of no—theoretical or political—use to see Greece as a "special case" or as a "guinea pig" that is sacrificed in order to be cured, as it is often said or reproduced by the media all over the world.[6] If we could patiently read history, we would see that the same signifiers, used to describe and explain the Greek bankruptcy and the *pathology* of the Greek economy, had *already* been used in the dominant discourse in Great Britain in the case of another "crisis", the "Famine Crisis" in Ireland more than 160 years ago, when a fungus, in 1845, attacked the potato crops, destroying them completely and causing an unprecedented decline in population due to death and migration (Neal 1998: 4). In both cases, "laziness" and "reluctance to modernization" were seen as the main causes for the crisis or the inability for a quick recovery. The Irish in 1847–48, as the Greeks in 2010, were described as "lazy" and "superstitious" (McLean 1999: 48); Ireland in mid-nineteenth century—just like Greece in twenty-first century—was a country with "lazy farmers", "slovenly" organised and with "people [who] had no incitement to be industrious" (Bigelow 2003: 119–122; Kinealy 2002: 91; see also Marx 1976: 854–870). Moreover, the signifiers used for migrants from Africa or Middle East were also used for the Irish who left their country and carried their poverty as a "virus" to wealthier countries. As we can read in a report in *Bristol Gazette*, on 25 February 1847: "This is no question of party, sect or class. All feel the pressure, all are interested. Through every pore is felt the exhausting drains of Irish distress and except the property of

zation of credit", which results in constructing calculable subjects, who aim at preserving and not overthrowing financial and social order (Bourdieu 2005).

[6] "Better to die from a bullet than working: That is the mantra of pampered, lazy Greek rioters used to living off the state". This was, for example, the headline of a reportage in *Daily Mail* only a few days after the voting of the "first memorandum" by the Greek parliament (Fernandes 2010).

Ireland is made to bear its share of Irish burdens, England will be dragged down to the level of Irish pauperism" (cited in Neal 1998: 242). A few decades later, at the other side of the Atlantic, where thousands of European migrants had been forced to move due to severe economic crisis in mid-nineteenth-century Europe, on the occasion of the Haymarket's events at Chicago, the fusion of humanist and capitalist crisis was inscribed in the front page of *Chicago Tribune*; only this time, the dangerous individuals were not migrants from Africa, Asia and Middle East, but from recently developed Northern Europe: Chicago had learned a bloody lesson; the "ungrateful hyenas" that had taken advantage of the tolerance of the locals should be deported and the "foreign savages who might come to America with their dynamite bombs and anarchic purposes" should be *excluded* (Green 2007: 8–9). It is pretty obvious that, as we have already mentioned, the fusion of a humanist and a capitalist crisis is as old as the discourse of capitalism itself. This fusion of crises, that is, the slippage to humanist discourse is the other side of the emergence of *racist* discourse, which is inherent in the bio-political discourse and practice of the capitalist system itself, as racism is not only or primarily an ideology, but a form of government designed to manage population in modernity (Foucault 2003) through the displacement of the sources of risk, dispossession and inequality from the capitalist regime to "inferior" groups of population, whose lack of incorporation and obedience to Capital's dictates and practices is a threat for the economic growth and prosperity of the whole society (Mavelli 2017).

Therefore, it is rather easy to understand that no humanist crisis or any crisis of moral values has erupted recently in Europe in general, or in Greece in particular; moreover, no humanist crisis or any crisis of moral values could explain, or even more, could be the cause of the capitalist crisis that burst in the West in 2007–8 and is still in full swing during the last decade. Rather, we are facing a *structural* function that has a long *history*: "What I have to examine in this work is the capitalist mode of production, and the relations of production and forms of intercourse that correspond to it. Until now, their *locus classicus* has been England. This is the reason why England is used as the main illustration of the theoretical developments I make. If, however, the German reader pharisaically shrugs his shoulders at the condition of the English industrial and agricultural workers, or optimistically comforts himself with the thought that in Germany things are not nearly so bad, I must plainly tell him: *De te fabula narratur*! [The tale is told of you!]" (Marx 1976: 90). Probably, Marx's warning about the tale that is told about everyone who lives, works and speaks within capitalist reality, whether s/he is British, German or Greek, was not expressed loudly enough, in order to be heard. That this structure is repeated throughout time, according to Marx, is well known by the opening phrase of *The 18th Brumaire of Louis Bonaparte*: "Hegel observes somewhere that all the great events and characters of world history occur twice, so to speak". Nevertheless, it is really crucial not to repeat the Hegelian oblivion, as Marx remarks in the very next sentence: "He forgot to add: the first time as high tragedy, the second time as low farce" (2002: 19). For, if we stay only at the level of ***repetition***, we repress that of ***difference***, since, firstly, in order to say that a historical fact is repeated there must be a difference in ***time***; secondly, the repetition that follows the event differs inevitably, according to Marx, in ***essence***, as "high tragedy" differs from "low farce" (ibid: 120,181). So, if we would like not to ***shrug our shoulders pharisaically*** to his warning, we should examine this structure's history, because it is not a tale told once and for all, but a reality constantly ***repeated*** in a ***different*** time and place, as the capitalist mode of production and consumption is expanding ***continuously*** throughout the world over the last three centuries, and its function is established in a ***different*** form. Thus, Marx's view of history is more complex and dynamic than the simplistic traditional concept of eternal and permanent repetition (Thucydides 2009: 12). If Marx's view was another version of the circular course of history, then the anticapitalist critique should be content to repeat monotonously and ascertain tediously that "crises are immanent to capitalism" and that these crises are "crises of human values", in the sense that, due to their systemic character, they are threatening the ability of human race to survive and the progress of Western civilisation (Robinson 2014: 5). However, even non-marxist political economists admit that there cannot be periods of growth that are not inevitably followed by periods of recession. Neoliberalism even anticipates crises in order to promote its policy (Mirowski 2013). Thus, maybe the radical character of the Marxian theory lies in the co-articulation of repetition ***and*** difference. It might be more radical, instead of asserting that capitalism generates crises, to raise the question of the difference in their repetition: how different is capitalism in the context of each new crisis? How different is each new crisis in the capitalist context of each historical conjuncture? Moreover, how does each crisis transform and re-construct human subjects that experience it?

If history's series of facts is a repetition, then a difference should emerge in their interpretation. If we would like to understand where exactly the *tragedy* and the *farce* of our own history lie, it might be better to raise questions regarding the *tragicomic* preconditions and consequences of economic, political, social and technological nexus of power *and* knowledge relations of our present. Namely, to raise questions regarding the historical conjuncture of the capitalist system that made possible for a tweet, sent on 23 April 2013 by Syrian hackers through *Associated Press'* tweet account, about a supposed explosion that injured Obama, to shake in *microseconds* the money markets leading to a tailspin of more than $130 billion of Standard & Poor's 500 value (Keller 2013; Prigg 2015). This event shows clearly not only the repetitive compulsion of the capitalist *standard* that the *poor* are constantly at risk to become poorer, since in a market economy every crash of this magnitude has severe effects in real economy, but also—and more significantly—that contemporary capitalist function has got rid of any illusion that market is a field of human freedom and choice. For, there was no room left for human intervention, as the transactions that led to the crash were ordered automatically by computers on the basis of algorithms used to analyse news circulated in social media (Karpi and Crawford 2016).

Thus, while Foucault, the so-called anti-humanist thinker, in his best-selling *tour de force* published in 1966 and titled *Les Mots et les choses* [*The Order of Things*] (Dosse 1998: 330–342), was wagering about Man's disappearance like a "face drawn in sand at the edge of the sea" (Foucault 1989: 422), a deeper historical process has *already* been underway in the fundamental arrangements of knowledge in the so-called societies of knowledge. For, Western subjectivities are not reflected anymore in the sand at the edge of the sea, but they are becoming more and more avatars reflected at the edge of the screens. At the heart of financial capitalism, at the stock exchanges' trading floors, a radical transition has taken place: "Even if traditional trading floors with busy human traders might still occupy a central place in the popular imagery of financial markets, their role in these markets has been greatly reduced. The buzz of traders yelling and pushing has been replaced by a set of new market actors – namely, fully automated computer algorithms that are programmed to execute trades under specific conditions" (Borch 2017). In Huizinga's terms, there are no gamblers playing in stock markets anymore, since these are functioning more and more like a computer game, eliminating thusly the distinction between human sovereign subjects and non-human instrumental objects. Consequently, it is time to turn our attention to the mode by which this *new order of things* is articulated, to the form through and by which *words and things* are related in modernity ...

References

Anderson, E. 2015. "Greece Crisis: Banks to Close on Monday and Capital Controls Imposed after ECB Caps Funding at Current Levels". http://www.telegraph.co.uk/finance/11704054/Greece-crisis-live-banks-to-close-on-Monday-and-capital-controls-imposed-after-ECB-caps-funding-at-current-levels.html (Accessed 15 July 2015).

Bátiz-Lazo, B., Efthymiou, L., and Michael, S. 2015. "When Payments Infrastructure Turns Political: The 2015 Greek Financial Crisis Through Social Lenses". http://www.charisma-network.net/finance/when-payments-infrastructure-turns-political-the-2015-greek-financial-crisis-through-social-lenses (Accessed 15 July 2017).

Bigelow, G. 2003. *Fiction, Famine, and the Rise of Economics in Victorian Britain and Ireland*. Cambridge/New York: Cambridge University Press.

Borch, C. 2017. "Algorithmic Finance and (Limits to) Governmentality: On Foucault and High-Frequency Trading." *Le foucaldien*, 3(1): 1–17. https://doi.org/10.16995/lefou.28.

Bourdieu, P. 2005. *The Social Structures of the Economy*, tr. C. Turner. Cambridge: Polity.

Bush, G. 2008. "Speech to the Nation on the Economic Crisis". http://www.nytimes.com/2008/09/24/business/economy/24text-bush.html?_r=0 (Accessed 17 February 2015).

Crouch, C. 2011. *The Strange Non-Death of Neo-liberalism*. Cambridge/Malden: Polity.

Dardot, P. and Laval, C. 2013. *The New Way of the World: On Neoliberal Society*, tr. G. Elliot. London/New York: Verso.

de Blic, D. and Lazarus, J. 2007. *Sociologie de l'argent*. Paris: La Decouverte.

de Grazia, M. 1999. "Teleology, Delay, and the 'Old Mole'". *Shakespeare Quarterly*, 50(3): 251–267.

Deleuze, G. 1992. "Postscript on the Societies of Control". *October*, 59: 3–7.

Derrida, J. 1994. *Spectres of Marx*, tr. P. Kamuf. London/New York: Routledge.

Dosse, F. 1998. *History of Structuralism. Vol. 1: The Rising Sign*, tr. D. Glassman. Minneapolis/London: University of Minnesota Press.

DW Staff. 2009. "French, German Leaders Call for 'Moralization' of Capitalism". http://www.dw.com/en/french-german-leaders-call-for-moralization-of-capitalism/a-3930542 (Accessed 22 September 2015).

Euromonitor 2017. "Financial Cards and Payments in Greece". http://www.euromonitor.com/financial-cards-and-payments-in-greece/report (Accessed 30 October 2017).

Efthymiou, L. and Michael, S. 2015. "The Cyprus Cash Crash: A Case of Collective Punishment". In B. Bátiz-Lazo. & L. Efthymiou (eds.), *The Book of Payments. Historical and Contemporary Views on the Cashless Society*. London: Palgrave Macmillan.

Fernandes, E. 2010. "Better to Die from a Bullet than Working: That is the Mantra of Pampered, Lazy Greek Rioters Used to Living Off the State". http://www.dailymail.co.uk/news/article-1275454/Better-die-bullet-working-Thatmantra-pampered-lazy-Greek-rioters-used-living-state.html (Accessed 30 October 2015).

Foucault, M. 1989. *The Order of Things: An Archaeology of the Human Sciences.* London/New York: Routledge.

Foucault, M. 2003. *"Society must be Defended". Lessons at the Collège de France, 1975–76*, tr. D. Macey. New York: Picador.

Foucault, M. 2007. *Security, Territory, Population. Lessons at the Collège de France, 1977–78*, tr. G. Burchel. New York: Palgrave Macmillan.

Fultner, B. 2014. *Jurgen Habermas – Key Concepts.* Oxon/New York: Routledge.

Green, J. 2007. *Death in the Haymarket: A Story of Chicago, the First Labor Movement and the Bombing that Divided Gilded Age America.* New York: Anchor.

Hanan, J.S. and Chaput, C. 2013. "Stating the Exception: Rhetoric and Neoliberal Governance During the Creation and Passage of the Emergency Economic Stabilization Act of 2008". *Argumentation and Advocacy,* 50(1): 18–33.

Harvey, D. 2010. *A Companion to Marx's Capital.* London/New York: Verso.

Hobsbawm, E. 1995. *The Age of Capital. 1848–75.* London: Abacus.

Huizinga, J.H. 1949. *Homo Ludens. A Study of the Play-Element in Culture.* London/Boston/Henley: Routledge & Kegan Paul.

Karatani, K. 2012. *History and Repetition.* New York: Columbia University Press.

Karpi, T. and Crawford, K. 2016. "Social Media, Financial Algorithms and the Hack Crash". *Theory, Culture & Society,* 33(1): 73–92. https://doi.org/10.1177/0263276415583139.

Katsourides, Y. 2016. *Radical Left Parties in Government. The Cases of SYRIZA and AKEL.* London: Palgrave Macmillan.

Keller, J. 2013. "A Fake AP Tweet Sinks the Dow for an Instant". https://www.bloomberg.com/news/articles/2013-04-23/a-fake-ap-tweet-sinks-the-dow-for-an-instant (Accessed 20 April 2016).

Kinealy, C. 2002. *The Great Irish Famine, Impact, Ideology and Rebellion.* London/New York: Macmillan.

Lazzarato, M. 2011. *The Making of the Indebted Man, An Essay on the Neoliberal Condition*, tr. J.D. Jordan. Amsterdam: Semiotext(e).

Leclerc, J.-J. 2006. *A Marxist Philosophy of Language*, tr. G. Elliott. Leiden/Boston: Brill.

Lih, T. 2008. *Lenin Rediscovered: What is to be Done? In Context.* Chicago: Haymarket Books.

Lih, T. 2011. *Lenin.* London: Reaktion Books.

Liu, H. L. 2010. "The Cybernetic Unconscious: Rethinking Lacan, Poe, and French Theory". *Critical Inquiry,* 36(2): 288–320.

Mavelli, L. 2017. "Governing the Resilience of Neoliberalism Through Biopolitics". *European Journal of International Relations*, 23(3): 489–512. https://doi.org/10.1177/1354066116676321.

Marx, K. 1976. *Capital, vol. 1*, tr. B. Fowkes. London: Penguin.

Marx, K. 2002. "The Eighteenth Brumaire". In M. Cowling and J. Martin (eds.), *Marx's Eighteenth Brumaire. (Post)modern Interpretations*. London: Pluto Press.

Marx, K. and Engels, F. 2012. *The Communist Manifesto: A Modern Edition*. London: Verso.

Maton, K. 2008. "Habitus: Introduction". In M.Grenfell (ed.), *Pierre Bourdieu. Key Concepts*. Durham: Acumen.

McLean, St. 1999. *The Event and Its Terrors: Ireland, Famine, Modernity*. California: Stanford University Press.

Miller, J.-A. 2002. "Milanese Intuitions". *Mental, International Journal of Mental Health and Applied Psychoanalysis*, 11: 9–16.

Mirowski, P. 2013. *Never Let a Serious Crisis Go to Waste How Neoliberalism Survived the Financial Meltdown*. London/New York: Verso.

Mudde, C. 2017. *SYRIZA, The Failure of the Populist Promise*. New York: Palgrave Macmillan.

Neal, F. 1998. *Black '47. Britain and the Famine Irish*. London: Palgrave Press.

Nietzsche, F. 1968. *The Will to Power*, tr. W. Kaufmann & R. J. Hollingdale. New York: Vintage House.

Nietzsche, F. 2006. *On the Genealogy of Morality*, tr. C. Diethe. Cambridge/New York: Cambridge University Press.

Online Etymology Dictionary. "Play". https://www.etymonline.com/word/play (Accessed 24 September 2017).

Online Etymology Dictionary. "Game". https://www.etymonline.com/word/game (Accessed 24 September 2017).

Online Etymology Dictionary "Gamble". https://www.etymonline.com/word/gamble (Accessed 24 September 2017).

Prigg M., (2015). "The Tweet that Cost $139 BILLION". http://www.dailymail.co.uk/sciencetech/article-3090221/The-tweet-cost-139-BILLION-Researchers-analyse-impact-hacked-message-claiming-President-Obama-injured-White-House-explosion.html (Accessed 20 May 2016).

Robat, C. 2006. "ATM. Automatic Teller Machine". *The History of Computing Project*. http://www.thocp.net/hardware/atm.htm (Accessed 22 July 2017).

Robinson, W.I. 2014. *Global Capitalism and the Crisis of Humanity*. New York: Cambridge University Press.

Rowell, D. and Conolly, L.B. 2012. "A History of the Term 'Moral Hazard'". *The Journal of Risk and Insurance*, 79(4): 1051–1075. https://doi.org/10.1111/j.1539-6975.2011.01448.x.

Serra, N. and Stiglitz, J.E (eds.), 2008. *The Washington Consensus Reconsidered. Towards a New Global Governance*. New York: Oxford University Press.

Shakespeare, W. 2005. *The Oxford Shakespeare: The Complete Works*. Oxford/New York: Oxford University Press.

Šumiç, J. 2016. "Politics and Psychoanalysis in Times of the Inexistent Other". In S. Tomŝiç and A. Zevnik (eds.), *Jacques Lacan. Between Psychoanalysis and Politics*. London/New York: Routledge.

The Telegraph. 2015. "Greeks Lose Their Love of Cash as Crisis Spurs Surge in Debit Cards". http://www.telegraph.co.uk/finance/economics/11782977/Greeks-lose-their-love-of-cash-as-crisis-spurs-surge-in-debit-cards.html (Accessed 20 September 2016).

Thucydides. 2009. *The Peloponnesian War*, tr. M. Hammond. London/New York: Oxford University Press.

Williams, M. 2010. *Uncontrollable Risk. Lessons of Lehman Brothers and How Systemic Risk Can Still Bring Down the World Financial System*. New York/London: McGraw Hill.

Žižek, S. 1989. *The Sublime Object of Ideology*. London/New York: Verso.

CHAPTER 9

The Man Without Qualities in a Universe Full of Quantities

Abstract Having as a starting point Robert Musil's masterpiece *The Man Without Qualities*, the tension between Enlightenment and Humanism is under discussion and examination. This tension is articulated as a linguistic clash between scientific and literary discourse and is inscribed onto the ec-*centric* character of modern subjectivity and the experience of "void" within the context of modern capitalist society. However, this ec-*centricity* is not merely subjective, but it is an objective characteristic of modern science and art, and a structural feature of the crisis of representation in both fields, as the historicalization of the crisis shows.

Keywords Musil • Representation crisis • Science • Art • Subject • 1913

15 April 1942: the Austrian author Robert Musil draws his last breath leaving incomplete his *magnum opus* entitled *The Man Without Qualities* (*Der Mann ohne Eigenschaften*) that he was writing for two decades, succeeding in seeing published only the first two volumes. Certainly, there is no exaggeration in the statement that this is one of the greatest novels of the twentieth century; one of the finest expressions of modernist literature, in consonance with other celebrated exponents of the movement, such as Mann, von Hofmannsthal, Broch, and Rilke (Payne 1988); a description and a query about the ec-*centric* character and the sense of

T. Lagios et al., *Borders, Bodies and Narratives of Crisis in Europe*,
https://doi.org/10.1007/978-3-319-75586-1_9

"void" that shapes the everyday experience of human subjects in the context of modern capitalist society (McBride 2006: 4–7; Dowden 1986). However, it could be seen as an exaggeration that this intricately woven novel of 1675 pages could be summarised by its very first chapter entitled ironically "From which, remarkably enough, nothing develops", as some have claimed (Spencer 2008: 16,152; Sebastian 2005: 53,80). If we would like to push exaggeration to its limits, we could suggest that it is not remarkable enough that nothing develops, since the opening paragraph summarises the hundreds of pages that follow, by drawing a noteworthy synopsis of the main *question* that agonises the novel's "hero" Ulrich, a 32-year-old mathematician, and the whole era. If this is the case, we should cite it in its entirety, in order to give the reader the opportunity to enjoy Musil's unique sense of humour and irony (Johnsson 2005: 159)—let us remind that, according to Lacan (Miller 2003), irony is "a weapon which goes to the heart of any social relation":

> A barometric low hung over the Atlantic. It moved eastward toward a high-pressure area over Russia without as yet showing any inclination to bypass this high in a northerly direction. The isotherms and isotheres were functioning as they should. The air temperature was appropriate relative to the annual mean temperature and to the aperiodic monthly fluctuations of the temperature. The rising and setting of the sun, the moon, the phases of the moon, of Venus, of the rings of Saturn, and many other significant phenomena were all in accordance with the forecasts in the astronomical yearbooks. The water vapor in the air was at its maximal state of tension, while the humidity was minimal. In a word that characterizes the facts fairly accurately, even if it is a bit old-fashioned: It was a fine day in August 1913. (Musil 1996: 3)

At this very point where the reader has been left rather perplexed due to the undoubtedly unconventional opening, a question arises: where exactly does Musil aim his weapon of irony, and what exactly is happening at the heart of social relations? Firstly, we should remark that the opening paragraph is literally divided, as the reader faces a linguistic clash (Rabaté 2007: 72) between a precise scientific account of the weather conditions bearing all the *positivist* marks of neutral objectivity, mathematical calculations and scientific detachment, and an "old-fashioned", traditional or literary description bearing all the *humanist* marks of subjectivism, personal taste and a Romantic sense of individuality. It is not hard to see that nearly the whole opening paragraph ignores our expectations from a novel and subverts any stylistic convention, since it is a faithful reproduction and an extensive account of an *objective*—modern, all too modern—meteorological report, instead of a *subjective* depiction under the anthropocentric perspective of the "hero" or, at least, the narrator. This highly anticipated perspective, usually performed by a standard opening clause, appears only at the final phrase, and only after it has been discredited as "old-fashioned", introducing "a discrepancy between an authoritative representation purporting to convey objective knowledge and a narrative mode accounting for the perspective of the particular individual" (Johnsson 2005: 150). Through the juxtaposition of the *detailed accuracy and precision* of the scientific measurement and calculation of the coordinates and relations between objects ("The isotherms and isotheres [...] of the temperature"), on the one hand, and the *sketchy subjective and individual* aesthetic and emotional judgement with the ambition to gain the status of an ontological statement ("it was a fine day"), on the other, Musil aims his weapon of irony at the very foundations of Western civilisation and modernity, as both discourses not only fail to fully re-present or clarify reality and its continuously and rapidly changing relation with human subject, but they also seem deeply incompatible. Thus, Musil introduces a *question* concerning the very roots of modern subjectivity, which is subjected to a historical condition, namely, a social, political, epistemological and economic conjuncture. If we would like to articulate and formulate this question as suitably as it should, we could not overlook that, as it has been aptly remarked, "*The Man without Qualities* exhausts battalions of received ideas and literary paradigms that once gave meaning to human existence. Its use of conventional narrative codes to wrap a content or an argument for which these conventions are insufficient creates comic effects that produce a state of indeterminacy, in which various discursive registers collide and are undone" (ibid: 158). The fact is that the discourse of Western societies seems so deeply divided between two ways of re-presenting reality that no attempt to bridge this division can be fruitful or meaningful.[1] For, mathematics and its equations have been the *lingua franca* of modern meteorology in particular and modern science in general (Cox 2002: 10), in full

[1] This exactly is the conclusion that Musil articulated in his first novel, entitled *The Confusions of Young Törless* (1906). As Musil's hero experiences: "Between events and himself, indeed, between his own emotions and some innermost self which craved that they be understood, there always remained a dividing line which retreated like a horizon from his yearning the closer he came to it" (2001: 25).

contrast to the well-worn signifiers of everyday language. This *lingua franca* emerged paradoxically at the heart of the Renaissance, since Galileo's ambition was to make clear that "the great book of the universe is written in mathematical language and its characters are triangles, circles, and other geometric figures" (cited in Milner 2000). As Koyré maintained, the mathematisation of science had two significant and interrelated characteristics: (a) the destruction of the *finite cosmos* of the Greek science, and (b) the geometrisation of space of the *infinite universe* of modern science and technique (Koyré 1957, 1965). Musil's question can now be raised: which is the appropriate interpretation of this fact, but, simultaneously and more importantly, which is the appropriate language and discourse that could aptly articulate the historical presuppositions and consequences of this conflict between the intellectual and the emotional human spheres?

However, a second—more crucial—question arises: which discourse prevails in the end? Before we hasten to answer, we should note that there is a deeper dichotomy underneath the aforementioned discursive conflict, emerging only through the *final* word of the paragraph [both in the German original and its English translation]; this word consists of four numbers: *1913*. Here, Musil seems to be inspired by Nietzsche's mistrust to any *theoretical* tool that ignores the question raised by the reality of hi*story* and the hi*story* of reality; by Nietzsche's mistrust to any perspective that looks for the Truth in the sphere of *Being* ignoring that of *Becoming*, thusly ignoring the very history and conventional character of the language it uses: "Everything else is deformity and pre-science: I mean metaphysics, theology, psychology, epistemology. *Or* formal science, a system of signs: like logic and that application of logic, mathematics. They do not have anything to do with reality, not even as a problem; they are equally distant from the question of whether a sign-convention like logic has any value at all" (2007a: 168). The concluding sign "1913" *punctuates* the whole opening paragraph, namely, in Lacan's words, produces its very meaning, since "the absence of punctuation is a source of ambiguity" (2006: 258,209). Thus, "1913" determines the paragraph's whole meaning and gives the coherence that seems to be lacking, as the linguistic clash disrupts the traditional narrative giving the impression of the mosaic of fragments. "1913" excludes ambiguity, on the one hand, as it interrupts the constellation of the dissimilar narrative registers, and emphasises, on the other, that we are less than a year before the assassination of Franz Ferdinand, the presumptive heir to the Habsburg throne, which triggered the outbreak of World War I. Explicitly, the four numbers interrupt the discursive discrepancy, by *grounding* its *cloudy* meaning, by questioning reality's relation with its re-presentation, since they emphasise that the novel starts at the very moment of what appears *in hindsight* as an impending (even predictable) crisis that would be fatal for Austria-Hungary, which would dissolve in its aftermath. A crisis that should be predictable to anyone in Austria-Hungary, since *already* in August *1913*, the second Balkan War had just ended bringing the Empire to the brink of war and setting the conditions for the general fighting of the next year (Hall 2000: 80–106). Anyone who reads the sign "1913" should feel bewildered by the hermeneutical confusion and inadequacy of the two opposing discourses and wonder if these sign-conventions have any value at all. For, "1913" reveals the inherent "perspectivism" of their understanding by asking ironically: what does the accumulation of mathematical descriptions of a day's ordinary processes show about that day in the course of human events? (Thiher 2005: 84). Thus, "1913" provokes the feeling that things themselves are inextricable from the codes in which they are articulated, but also reveals an inconsistency between the alarming tones of *history* and reassuring re-presentations, such as "in accordance with the forecasts" or "it was a fine day". We should remark here that Musil gives the impression that he emphasises particularly the dimension of *time* in the detriment of the dimension of space: "So let us not place any particular value on the city's name. [...] Time was on the move. People not yet born in those days will find it hard to believe, but even then time was racing along like a cavalry, camel, just like today. But nobody knew where time was headed" (1996: 4–7). However, this does not mean that he ignores the dimension of space; on the contrary, he makes a particular use of *space* where his story develops, since he constantly uses a metonymy ("Kakania") instead of the city's name. We should remark here that Musil's irony uses the metonymy "Kakania" as a reference to Vienna, "a scatological pun on the official Austro-Hungarian abbreviation *k.k.* [*kaiserlich-königlich* empire]", in an attempt to signify the lack of an encompassing system in a culture so entrapped in the inherited and invented fictions and images of itself, that cannot understand the essential instability that its very signifier represents: *Imperial and Royal, Austrian and Hungarian*, namely, an "absurd anachronism" (Dowden 1986: 57–8; Zaller 2005: 106). This anachronism is inscribed on the metonymy of an Empire's capital city that lacks a *central* will power and ability to generate a purpose and a leading idea in order to provide social cohesion (Tayler-Turner 2014: 93). The metonymic alliteration (*k.k.*) symbolises an absurd anachronism, just like putting the *literary* phrase "it is a fine day" *after* the detailed *scientific* description of the sky.

Thus, the opening paragraph's final sign forces us to recognise Musil's insight that *neither* the scientific or positivist discourse, *nor* the discourse of literature or humanism, can fully re-present or signify the whole reality or the relation between the human subject and the world in a historical conjuncture of crisis. Musil's insight, inscribed onto the sign "1913", is not only that scientific objectivity and subjective experience are two incompatible approaches to the world, but, more crucially, that this disjunction is not the main factor for science's inability to forecast the future and for art's inability to understand life. Musil's punctuation of the linguistic conflict with the sign "1913" shows that scientific discourse not only lacks any *pro-gnostic* power, but it also does not serve as a *foundation* of meaning, if it is used outside of its field as a guiding line for society, as positivists claimed; or, as a re-presentation of historical process, as it could not *pre*-dict the storm that would sweep Europe and the whole world, despite its precise and detailed calculations and its ambition for objective account of the reality and forecasting of dangers and risks.[2] "1913" reveals that the whole amassing of meteorological data is calming and reassuring about what is happening, but at the same time ends up being deceptive and misleading about what is going to happen in the near future, repressing the interrelation and the entanglement between present and future with the *past*. History reveals that the subjects of that discourse were also subjected to its positivist perspective, ignoring *history* itself and the field of *Becoming*. Looking at the sky is not the best perspective, if we would like to understand what is happening on the earth, as Nietzsche claimed criticising both the Platonic theory of Forms and the Kantian moral theory.[3] With a colourful metonymy, Nietzsche attacked this idealistic perspective: "it is quite clear which color is a hundred times more important for a genealogist than blue: namely *grey*, which is to say, that which can be documented, which can actually be confirmed and has actually existed, in short, the whole, long, hard-to-decipher hieroglyphic script of man's moral past!" (2006: Preface, §7).

[2] It is not surprising that Husserl developed these themes in the 1930s in the *Crisis of European Sciences and Transcendental Phenomenology*.

[3] Plato in *Phaedrus* located the place of the archetypal Forms "on the outer edge of heaven" (Plato 2002: 247b-c) and Kant concludes his *Critique of Practical Reason* with a celestial metaphor: "Two things fill the mind with ever new and increasing admiration and reverence, the more often and more steadily one reflects on them: the starry heavens above me and the moral law within me" (Kant 2015: 129).

However, Vilhelm Bjerknes, one of the founders of weather forecasting, declared in his inaugural lecture at the new Institute of Geophysics in Leipzig in *1913* that he preferred the sky's shining *blue* than historical archives' dusty *grey*, in order to *pre*-dict the future: "What is it that I really seek? Whither am I steering? I could not free myself from the thought that 'there is after all but one problem worth attacking, viz, the precalculation of future conditions'" (cited in Nebeker 1995: 90). Yet, Bjerknes was—as every knowing subject—so inevitably immersed and embedded in history, that even his scientific terminology of the celestial phenomena was entangled with the phenomena that were taking place underneath: when he discovered the presence of moving boundaries that separated warm and cold air masses, he used a *wartime* analogy and labelled the boundaries as "fronts", according to the current political climate (Henson 2010: 6). In 1913, Bjerknes with Lewis Fry Richardson, an English meteorologist, worked out a scheme for computing the weather, which ended up in 1922 in a book explicitly entitled *Weather Prediction by Numerical Process*. The title was really ambitious, as early-twentieth-century positivist meteorologists tried through their models of calculus and equation sets to lay the foundations of *forecasting* and eventually *controlling* weather that only a technological innovation could materialise: the electronic digital computer. Richardson admitted that "[64,000 human] computers would be needed to race the weather for the whole globe" and, as von Neumann himself remarked in the Meteorology Project's Justification Memorandum, "[the Project would take] the first steps toward influencing the weather by rational, human intervention … since the effects of any hypothetical intervention will have become calculable" (Harper 2008: 1–10). However, even several decades later, and despite the impressive and rapid developments in computer technology, the "forecast factory", as Richardson envisaged (Cox 2002: 157), still remains at the world of "more or less", instead of the universe of "precision" (Stewart 2002: 116–8).[4] Consequently, despite the eloquently articulated belief that meteorological science had conquered—empirically and theoretically—the goal to calculate and predict future weather conditions with enviable precision, histori-

[4]As Koyré claimed, the deepest meaning and aim of the Scientific Revolution "of which Newton is the heir and the highest expression, is just to abolish the world of the 'more or less', the world of qualities and sense perception, the world of appreciation of our daily life, and to replace it by the (Archimedean) universe of precision, of exact measures, of strict determination" (1965: 4–5).

cal contingency emerges at the very heart of science. For, even sky, that is, our description of the sky, has its own history, its own relation between nature and culture. Thus, there is no *sky* (*ciel*, in French) separable from the social underneath. The way each society in each historical conjuncture observes and describes sky is always a soci*al* phenomenon determined by and, at the same time, determining the "soci*el*", since "the agricultural civilization finds its bearings in Nature, in the invariable cycle of seasons. [...] The agricultural real is celestial; it is a friend of nature. With industry, with what we call the industrial revolution, all that was slowly swept away. The artifices were multiplied and now we are forced to notice that the real is devouring nature, that it is being substituted for it and is proliferating (Miller 2004).

Musil, a trained mathematician and engineer, already from *1913* in his essay entitled "The Mathematical Man", had raised questions regarding the repercussions from the fact that the very foundations of the mathematical formalisation of modern science are standing *on the air*, while their products are functioning perfectly transforming deeply the *face of the earth*: "For the pioneers of mathematics formulated usable notions of certain principles that yielded conclusions, methods of calculation, and results, and these were applied by the physicists to obtain new results; and finally came the technicians, who often took only the results and added new calculations to them, and thus the machines arose. And suddenly, after everything had been brought into the most beautiful kind of existence, the mathematicians–the ones who brood entirely within themselves–came upon something wrong in the fundamentals of the whole thing that absolutely could not be put right. They actually looked all the way to the bottom and found that the whole building was standing in midair. But the machines worked!" (cited in McBride 2006: 53–54). Musil follows Nietzsche's scepticism regarding the modern faith in progress, especially in the field of knowledge or in what modernity calls "science": "We call it 'explanation', but 'description' is what distinguishes us from older stages of knowledge and science. We are better at describing – we explain just as little as all our predecessors" (2007b: §112). This scepticism was confirmed in the twentieth century by scientists, who challenged Snow's insurmountable dividing line between two cultures.[5]

[5] Plotnitsky discusses critically "Snow's divide" and the consequent asymmetry in the discussion between scientific discourse and discourse of art or humanities (Plotnitsky 2002). Nobelist Erwin Schrödinger had warned, ten years before Snow, in a lecture entitled "Science

Thus, he avoids the positivist stance that the overcoming of this impasse could only come, when the scientific discourse conquers the discursive field against the "natural Luddites", namely, the intellectuals of human sciences, as C.P. Snow claimed in a 1959 famous lecture (Snow 1998; Plotnitsky 2002).

However, Musil also avoids the technophobic discourse of historical nostalgia inspired by Plato (Dowden 1986: 27–56), as his modernism differs from that of Broch's or Mann's (Kundera 2003: 47–70; 1996: 160–164). As it has been remarked, "Musil's reflections are perfectly inscribed within the epochal debate about the relationships between *Kultur* and *Zivilisation*. In the *corpus* of Musil's works, the dichotomy between emotion and intellect assume diverse ramifications that are divided between imagination and reality, faith and knowledge, spirituality and exactitude, and morals and science" (Larese 2015). Consequently, the significance and distinctiveness of Musil's question and stance against the problem of division or gap between the positivist or scientific and the humanist or literary discourse is not that he opts for the one against the other, but that he describes the historical and structural impasse, where the blind faith in both discourses characterises people in Western societies (Johnsson 2005: 170).[6] Here, he anticipates also Foucault's view regarding the proper function of literature, which, according to Foucault, has a very recent history, namely, since the nineteenth century, when literature acquired its self-reflective perspective: "So that asking the question 'What is literature?' became indistinguishable from the act of writing itself. [...] It's almost as if a cavity had been opened up within literature, a cavity in which the question resides and can gather together its entire being"

and Humanism", against the blind faith in scientists regarding philosophical questions; namely, against technocracy: "The majority of educated persons are not interested in science, and are not aware that scientific knowledge forms part of the idealistic background of human life. Many believe—in their complete ignorance of what science really is—that it has mainly the ancillary task of inventing new machinery, or helping to invent it, for improving our conditions of life. They are prepared to leave this task to the specialists, as they leave the repairing of their pipes to the plumber" (2014: 113).

[6] Musil should be distinguished from Jefrey Herf's category of "reactionary modernism" (Herf 1998), since he emphasised not the incorporation of the two poles, but the structural division between *Kultur* and *Zivilization*, suggesting the impasse of privileging either German nationalism or Western technology and scientific modernity. If reactionary modernists faced the dilemma *Kultur or Zivilization* by answering *Kultur and Zivilization*, Musil's modernism consists in raising a question regarding the *historical presuppositions and repercussions of the relation between dilemma's terms.*

(2015: 45).[7] This cavity within language is the cavity that opened up by Musil's irony and perspicacity to set the action at Vienna in 1913, at the heart of Europe, at the capital city of a descending Empire, and in a historical moment, when almost everything anticipated the approaching disaster of World War I, in order to articulate a question regarding the interpretation of the impending crisis in the West: what kind of human being, namely, what kind of subjectivity is constituted in a historical conjuncture, in which not only the most modern language, but also the most old-fashioned, fail to describe what is really happening during the most critical times?

In order to answer this question, we should examine the historical *a priori* and consequences of the crisis of modern science and art concerning human subjectivity; we should examine the irony of Musil's punctuation with the sign "1913", "aiming at the heart of social relation", showing that a deeper dichotomy exists in *science's* domain, where a crisis had *already* been emerging, a crisis that "radically redefined the nature of knowledge by making the unknowable an irreducible part of knowledge" (Plotnitsky 2002: xiii), and also in *art's* domain, where a crisis of aesthetic representation and of art itself had *already* been emerging, leading to an identity crisis (Witham 2013). Consequently, there should be no surprise, that "from there nothing develops", according to the chapter's title; or that a *Man Without Qualities* fully emerged both in the field of science and art, according to the novel's title.

In the field of *science*, Musil's question forebodes the Lacanian position for the subject of science and its relation to the subject of the unconscious,[8] which, as J.-C. Milner suggests, is founded on Koyré's epistemology and Kozève's historical perspective. For, modern science, that is, *mathematicised* science after Galileo, "calculates the empirical as such, without converting it into Forms and Numbers. The necessity of its reasonings does

[7] It is worth noting that Musil and his *magnum opus* were so deeply admired by Foucault, that Hervé Guibert, one of Foucault's close friends, in his *roman à clef* entitled *To the Friend Who Did Not Save My Life* named the book character identifying with Foucault as "Muzil" (sic). See, Miller (1993: 165,170).

[8] Lacan described the relation between the subject of science and of the unconscious in contemporary society where *Knowledge* becomes the *Master Signifier* as follows: "Who, in our day, is capable of dreaming even for an instant of arresting the movement of articulation of the discourse of science in the name of anything at all that could come out of it? [...]Don't think that the master is always there. It's the command that remains the categorical imperative, 'Keep on knowing'. There is no longer any need for anybody to be present. We have, as Pascal says, all embarked upon the discourse of science" (2007: 104–6).

not share a connaturality with the necessity of the Ideas. It requires no soul, and, even if the soul exists, it demands nothing from it" (Milner 1996–7). The difference between the ancient Greek science and the modern one is that, after Galileo and what is called the "Scientific Revolution", in modernity "physics eliminates every quality from existents, therefore a theory of the subject that wishes to respond to such a physics must also strip the subject of every quality. This subject, constituted following the characteristic determinations of science, is the subject of science". Thus, modern subject is actually based on—and, at the same time, produces—a subject without *qualities*, for "the qualitative markings of the empirical individual are not appropriate to the subject, whether they are somatic or psychic, nor are the qualitative properties of a soul. The subject is neither mortal nor immortal, neither pure nor impure, neither just nor unjust, neither sinner nor saint, neither damned nor saved. Even the properties that for a long time have been believed to constitute subjectivity as such are not appropriate: this subject has neither self, nor reflexivity, nor consciousness" (Milner 2000: 38). Aristotle's emphasis on the nonconformity of mathematical concepts to the data of sense-experience and of the inability of mathematics to explain quality and to deduce movement was subverted by the emergence of a physical, or rather, mechanical system which was implicitly present in the arguments of Copernicus (Koyré 1943). How was this shift possible? According to Koyré, this became possible due to the epistemological relation between modern physics and astronomy. Thanks to the infamous Copernican Revolution that placed Sun at the centre and set Earth in motion, modern science was based on serious epistemological presuppositions: "the replacement of the classic and medieval conception of the *Cosmos*–closed unity of a qualitatively determined and hierarchically well ordered whole in which different parts (heaven and earth) are subject to different laws–by that of the *Universe*, that is of an open and indefinitely extended entirety of Being, governed and united by the identity of its fundamental laws; [...] implying the impossibility of establishing and elaborating a terrestrial physics, or, at least, a terrestrial mechanics, without a celestial one"(ibid). However, this replacement of Earth by Sun, signified by the signifier "heliocentrism", was not the real revolution, as Kant and Freud, among many others, believed. According to Lacan, the real revolution, namely, the radical change was Keplerian, not Copernican: "The Copernican revolution is by no means a revolution. If the center of a sphere is assumed, in a discourse that is merely analogical, to constitute the pivotal point (*point-maître*), the fact of changing this pivotal point, of having it be occupied by the earth or the sun, involves nothing that in itself subverts what the signifier 'center' intrinsically (*de lui-même*) preserves. Man – what is designated by this term, which is nothing but that which makes (things) signify – was far from ever having been shaken by the discovery that the earth is not at the center. He had no problem substituting the sun for it. [...] Of course it is now obvious that the sun is not a center either, and that it is strolling through a space whose status is ever more precariously established. What remains at the center is the fine routine that is such that *the signified always retains the same meaning (sens)* in the final analysis. [...] What is crucial, as some people have noticed, is not Copernicus, but more specifically Kepler, due to the fact that in his work it does not turn in the same way – it turns in an *ellipse*, and that *already throws into question the function of the center.* That toward which it falls in Kepler's work is a point of the ellipse that is called a focus, and in the symmetrical point there is nothing. That is assuredly a corrective to the image of the center" (1999: 42–3; emphasis added). Shortly, the radical change in the relation between the human subject and the universe took place, when the *elliptical* form replaced the *circular* and when *infinite* replaced *finite.* Modernity became a synonym of crisis, since human subjects were displaced from the *centre* of a finite and harmonic *world* to the ec-*centric* position of an infinite and chaotic *universe.*

This crisis was represented in the mathematisation of science; as Milner aptly summarised this historical process, crisis was articulated in scientific discourse and was accelerated by its dire consequences: "[f]irst of all that mathematics, in science, can spell out all the empirical, without concerning itself with any hierarchy of being, without ordering the objects on a scale going from the least perfect—intrinsically rebellious to number—to the most perfect—almost entirely numerable; second, it is that mathematics, spelling out the entirety of the empirical, intervenes by means of its literal nature, that is via calculation, rather than by demonstration (the emergence of science is also the inexorable decline of *mos geometricus*); third, it is that mathematics spells out the empirical as such, in its passing, its imperfection and its opacity. One then understands the articulation of science with technique" (2000: 45–46). Namely, after the universe's mathematisation, which paradoxically began at the heart of the Renaissance establishing the modern worldview and rationality, firstly, the rejection of any hierarchy of *Being* renders humanist slogans such as "People over profit", simply meaningless or non-sensical; secondly, the priority of *calculation* renders workers plainly and simply "units of value" or, in more modern terms, in the contemporary "information societies", where workers are students in a "lifelong learning" process and "24/7" consumers through debit and credit cards, everyone is represented by "credit points"; lastly, all these processes are symbolised and quantified mathematically under the pretext of objectivity. Hence, the modern epistemological shift has left its imprint on modern subjectivity, as a Man *without Qualities* corresponds *precisely* to a Universe *full of Quantities.* This imprint was eloquently inscribed onto the very title of one of the foundational texts of our era of digital communication and information; Claude Shannon's "The Mathematical Theory of Communication" (1948) showed the displacement from quality to quantity at the level of what was—till then—considered as the essentially *human* activity: communication. Digitally speaking, Shannon attempted a separation of the *meaning* of communication from the technical or more specifically mathematical problem of communication's *transmission*. As Nikolas Gane remarks, "Shannon and Weaver's solution is to conceive of information in terms of choice and uncertainty, and, in line with this, treat communication as a question of probability rather than of semantics" (2005). Here, a question arises: how did it become possible to give primacy to the *technical* problem of communication over the question of its meaning? Have we not entered, at this point, both technically *and* theoretically, to wit, *techno-logically* the gates of post-humanism?

If we turn our gaze to history, in order to see—very shortly, and rather schematically—how this process resulted in "the Turing game", where "Man coincides with his simulation" (Kittler 1999: 17), we should mention that firstly a paradox should be resolved, as "at the origin of Galilean science, [...] the moment this science declares itself mathematized and refers the universe to the infinite, there is no mathematics of the infinite" (Milner 1996–7). This revolution in mathematics was absolutely necessary, because great mathematicians "like Gauss, Euler, Jacobi, Abel, and others of the founding fathers of modern mathematics not only did not base their work on the yet-to-be-invented theory of sets, they based it on an altogether different conception of mathematics, one which explicitly *excluded* completed infinites" (Edwards 1995: 50; emphasis added). Gauss, the legendary "Prince of mathematicians", belonging to the pre-industrial sociel (Buhler 1981: 11–14), had warned his colleagues of the dire consequences of the inclusion of the infinite in mathematics: "I protest above all against the use of an infinite quantity as a completed one, which in mathematics is never allowed. The infinite is only a manner of speaking, in which one properly speaks of limits" (cited in Davis 2000: 60).[9] Nevertheless, as the sociel was becoming industrial and as the capitalist relations of productions were expanding all over the world, this kind of metaphysics that respected the limits of human experience regarding space became obsolete. Riemann, guided extensively by Gauss's intrinsic geometry of surfaces in Euclidean space, developed an intrinsic geometry for *any* space (Kline 1972: 871–890). Thusly, as Deleuze has remarked, Leibnizian monadology, after Riemann's differential and non-Euclidean geometry, resulted in the construction of a *God without qualities* (Deleuze 1993: 81).[10]

How could a subject, either a man or a woman, either human or divine, exist and communicate in a world without qualities that is represented not in Euclidean geometry's terms, but according to an n-dimensional infinite order? As Leibniz had claimed, there was a need for a universal language, based on binary notation (0 & 1) that would be useful in laying bare properties of numbers that otherwise would be hidden. Frege had the courage to make the attempt to fulfil Leibniz's dream. In 1879, he published his *Begriffsschrift*, ("conceptual notation"); it was subtitled "a formula language, modeled upon that of arithmetic, for pure thought". In fact, *Begriffsschrift* was "the ancestor of all computer programming languages in common use today" (Davis 2000: 15–19; 48–53). His intention was "not to represent an abstract logic in formulas, but to express a content through written signs in a more precise and clear way than it is possible to do through words. In fact, what I wanted to create was not a mere *calculus ratiocinator* but a *lingua characterica* in Leibniz's sense" (cited in Heijenoort 1967: 5). However, as Russell showed and Frege admitted, even the most strictly scientific discourse could not avoid a paradox at the very heart of its enterprise, an enterprise that was supportive to Cantor's

[9] Leibniz, one of the co-inventors of infinitesimal calculus, made the first attempt to invent a universal language, in order to symbolise mathematically the new method of calculation of infinitesimals. This calculus demanded infinite and imaginary numbers that Leibniz characterised as follows: "Imaginary roots are a subtle and wonderful resort of the divine spirit, a kind of hermaphrodite between existence and non-existence" (cited in Plotnitsky 2002). Gauss, in his turn, warned in 1825 that "the true metaphysics of the square root of -1 remains elusive" (cited in Berlinski 2008: 79).

[10] As Berlinski remarks, "if there is one abstract space, and that one capable of incarnating itself in various ways, then the question of whether the space in which we live is Euclidean, elliptical, or hyperbolic, or even some unsuspected monstrosity in between, is no longer mathematical" (2008: 121–2).

embrace of the actual infinite and cardinal numbers (Davis 2000: 60; Boyer and Merzbach 2011: 522–525). This paradox could be summarised in the following question: *Can there be a set of all sets?* (Davis 2000: 77). Lacan summarised the crisis, since "mathematics is constructible only on the basis of the fact that the signifier is capable of signifying itself. The *A* that you have written down on one occasion can be signified by its repetition as *A*. Now, this position is strictly untenable, it constitutes a violation of the rules with respect to the function of the signifier, which can signify anything except, surely, itself. It is this initial postulate that one must throw off in order for the discourse of mathematics to get started" (2007: 90). Or, as Russell commented on the inconsistency and the lack of verifiability lying at the heart of scientific discourse's tautological character, "mathematics may be defined as the subject in which we never know what we are talking about, nor whether what we are saying is true" (cited in Greenshields 2017: 148). This tautological character of scientific discourse is possible, since "the letter is not a more refined representation of the celestial thing-in-itself, it instead replaces this thing". Thusly, "the theoretical physicist can arrive at laws and consequences by working with equations and formulae long before these same results are finally verified by empirical experimentation" (ibid).[11]

If we recall Musil's punctuation of "1913", further questions are raised, as Russell and Whitehead published that very year the final volume of their *Principia Mathematica*, where they tried to prove that all of pure mathematics can be derived from a small number of fundamental logical principles, based on a theory of classes that was safe from the paradoxes. However, in 19*31* (an interesting, for every Pythagorean, numerical transposition) "the young Austrian mathematician Kurt Gödel showed that within a rigidly logical system, such as Russell and Whitehead had developed for arithmetic, propositions can be formulated that are undecidable or undemonstrable within the axioms of the system" (Boyer and Merzbach 2011: 560). Moreover, in the field of physics, crisis was deepening, as Einstein, who in 1913 was voted for membership in the Prussian Academy of Sciences (Miller 2001: 228), published with Grossmann a paper enti-

[11] Here, we could recall Musil's opening and relate it to Wittgenstein's remark in *Tractatus* regarding the tautological character of language and the problem of speaking and representing Truth: "For example, I know nothing about the weather when I know that it is either raining or not raining" (Wittgenstein 2001: 4.461). Moreover, Wittgenstein characterises Frege's *Begriffsschrift* a "mechanical expedient" as a proof that a proposition is either a tautology or a contradiction (McManus 2006: 85).

tled "Outline of a Generalized Theory of Relativity and of a Theory of Gravitation", to develop a theory that would generalise the relativity of uniform motion of special relativity to arbitrary accelerated motion (Jansen and Lehner 2014: 14). It was the very same year, when Niels Bohr published his famous "Trilogy" describing a new theory of atoms that obliged "physicists after 1913 to exert themselves on the dual task of expanding our knowledge of atomic phenomena while carrying out a radical and, in some ways, then unpredictable revision of the foundations of physics" (Petruccioli 1994: 37). This debate took place not only on strictly scientific terms, since the clash between physicists was also aesthetic, as two modes of *representation* were at stake: the wave representation for electrons, with its visual imagery and associated continuous and hopefully causal description of atomic physics, and the particle representation, with its inherent discontinuities, lack of visualisation and questionable causality (Miller 2001: 256).

Thus, it is time to move to the field of *art*, since Musil's irony, as we have already mentioned, shows that this crisis had emerged in the artistic discourse, too. 1913 was an emblematic year regarding the crisis of aesthetic representation, as Marcel Proust rocked the muddy waters beginning the first volume of his masterpiece *In Search of Lost Time* with the notorious opening phrase "For a long time I used to go to bed early", resulting in the subversion of narrative's linear structure (Watt 2011: 44–45), since the novel's first-person narrator is "at once the hero participating in the events recalled and an older narrator looking back upon a younger version of himself in time past" (Thiher 2005: 102). Proust's construction of a chaotic temporal flux followed the end of classical determinism, as it was undermined by Henri Poincaré's dynamical system theory and its impact on rendering obvious the crisis of science and mathematics at the beginning of the century (ibid: 105; Parker 2007: 61–86). At the same year and under the same influence, Marcel Duchamp subverted the established aesthetic order by presenting the first "readymade", which was a banal and hackneyed product of mass and technical reproduction presented as a work of art: a bicycle wheel on a kitchen stool raising the question of doing works without doing art (Moffitt 2003: 225–264). Art was under crisis, since it followed the very path that science and technology had already paved. The artistic representation was subverted by *mechanical reproduction*, as photography, moving pictures, gramophone recordings and Marconi's wireless transmission were realised due to electricity (Gale 1997: 27). Duchamp was clear about this transposition from the order of *senses* to that of *machines*: "The movement of form in time inevitably ushered us into geometry and mathematics. It's the same as when you build a machine" (Cabanne 1987: 31). Picasso and the Cubists were also at the same wave of thought, as Maurice Princet, an amateur mathematician and insurance adjustor, initiated them along with Duchamp into Poincaré's work and the debates regarding non-Euclidean geometry, the measurement of curved space and the mysterious "fourth dimension" (Witham 2013: 44–6; Bodish 2009). Artists were interested in these debates regarding the inability of human senses to fully perceive and understand reality and its phenomena in an infinite and manifold space-time (Henderson 2009). This interest was expressed, in 1913, when the *Armory Show* also took place in New York, where Duchamp presented his *Nude Descending the Staircase* and Picasso his *Woman with Mustard Pot*, raising a scandal, as they were considered an affront to civilisation (Witham 2013: 1–5). Duchamp claimed that his work was, perhaps unconsciously, an example of the use of Étienne-Jules Marey's invention of chronophotography, in order to give the idea of the *mechanisation* of man as opposed to *perceptible beauty* (Cabanne 1987: 33), while Picasso was dethroning perspective in painting following technological inventions of his time, like X-rays (Miller 2001) and the fourth-dimensional geometry (Robbin 2006). Both were in the right place at the right time: in 1913, New York, except *Armory Show*, saw the mechanically reproduced art of film founding its temple at the Regent Theatre, the first luxurious theatre exclusively for films and movies (Belton 2013: 16). At this point, since we made a reference to cinema, we should note the following historical detail: on 25 July 1913, during the second Balkan War, Romanian aviators took pictures of Sofia from their planes and dropped leaflets for the population (Rabaté 2007: 7). Sofia was thus not only the first European capital city to come under the wings of enemy aircraft, but also the first European capital city to be captured by the camera by air during war, confirming Kittler's statement that "[t]he history of the movie camera thus coincides with the history of automatic weapons", as Marey invented the first serial-shot camera, which was described as a "chronophotographic rifle", since "the transport of pictures only repeats the transport of bullets" (Kittler 1999: 123–4). Hence, it is the very technological structure of modernity that provoked a crisis in artistic representation, despite the zealous efforts of the artistic subjects to express their human essence or their "inner world" criticising dehumanised external reality by representing reality by and for Man.

For, at the twilight of the *belle époque*, a dizzying sequence of breakthroughs provoked a crisis that neither art nor science seemed able to overcome or even *re*-present, as quantum physics demonstrated that the crisis of representation was at the heart of science and art alike. As it has been claimed, abstraction and indeterminacy entered the scene blurring the picture, by emphasising the limits of our perception, while, at the same time, erased the limits between scientific and artistic representation: "Feynman diagrams represent a world beyond the forms to which our perceptions restrict us. They are the most abstract scientific art existing today. The only barrier to further abstraction is that we must still represent a figure separate from its background. Thus, we cannot represent or imagine something that is a wave and particle simultaneously. But subatomic particles are just that, and Feynman diagrams are presently our only means to view them in a way consistent with their properties" (Miller 2001: 261). Consequently, it should be no surprise that the Nobelist physicist Werner Heisenberg raised the crucial—Nietzschean—question regarding the problem of reality and the sign-convention system of its representation as follows: "The improved experimental technique of our time brings into the scope of science new aspects of nature which cannot be described in terms of the common concepts. But in what language, then, should they be described?" (1958: 167–8).

References

Belton, J. 2013. *American Cinema, American Culture.* New York: McGraw Hill.
Berlinski, D. 2008. *Infinite Ascent: A Short History of Mathematics.* New York: Modern Library.
Bodish, E. 2009. "Cubism and the Fourth Dimension". *The Montana Mathematics Enthusiast*, 6(3): 527–540.
Boyer, C.B. and Merzbach, U.C. 2011. *A History of Mathematics.* Hoboken, NJ: Wiley.
Buhler, W.K. 1981. *Gauss, A Biographical Study.* Berlin/Heidelberg/New York: Springer.
Cabanne, P. 1987. *Dialogues with Marcel Duchamp*, tr. R. Padgett. London: Da Capo Press.
Cox, J.D. 2002. *Storm Watchers. The Turbulent History of Weather Prediction from Franklin's Kite to El Niño.* New Jersey: John Wiley & Sons.
Davis, M. 2000. *Engines of Logic, Mathematicians and the Origin of the Computer* London/New York: W.W. Norton and Co.

Deleuze, G. 1993. *The Fold. Leibniz and the Baroque*, tr. T. Conley. London: Athlone Press.

Dowden, S. D. 1986. *Sympathy for the Abyss, A study in the Novel of German Modernism: Kafka, Broch, Musil and Thomas Mann*. Tubingen: M. Niemayer.

Edwards, H. M. 1995. "Kronecker on the Foundations of Mathematics". In J. Hintika (ed.), *From Dedekind to Gödel. Essays on the Foundations of Mathematics*. Netherlands: Springer.

Foucault, M. 2015. *Language, Madness, Desire*. Minneapolis/London: University of Minnesota Press.

Gale, M. 1997. *Dada and Surrealism*. London/New York: Phaedon Press.

Gane, N. 2005. "Radical Post-humanism. Friedrich Kittler and the Primacy of Technology". *Theory, Culture & Society*, 22(3): 25–41. https://doi.org/10.1177/0263276405053718.

Greenshields, W. 2017. *Writing the Structures of the Subject. Lacan and Topology*. New York: Palgrave Macmillan.

Hall, R.C. 2000. *The Balkan Wars 1912–3. Prelude to the First World War*. London/New York: Routledge.

Harper, K. 2008. *Weather by the Numbers. The Genesis of Modern Meteorology*. Cambridge, MA/London: MIT Press.

Heijenoort, J.V. 1967. *From Frege to Gödel, A Source Book in Mathematical Logic, 1879–1931*. Cambridge, MA: Harvard University Press.

Henderson, L.D. 2009. "The Image and Imagination of the Fourth Dimension in Twentieth-Century Art and Culture". *Configurations*, 17(1): 131–160.

Herf, J. 1998. *Reactionary Modernism Technology, Culture, and Politics in Weimar and the Third Reich*. Cambridge, UK: Cambridge University Press.

Heisenberg, W. 1958. *Physics and Philosophy, The Revolution in Modern Science*. New York: Harpers and Brothers Publishing.

Henson, R. 2010. *Weather on the Air. A History of Broadcast Meteorology*. Boston: American Meteorology Society.

Jansen, M. and Lehner, C. 2014. *The Cambridge Companion to Einstein*. New York: Cambridge University Press.

Johnsson, S. 2005. "A Story with Many Ends: *Narratological Observations*". In H. Bloom (ed.), *Robert Musil's The Man without Qualities*. Philadelphia: Chelsea House.

Kant, I. 2015. *Critique of Practical Reason*, tr. M. Gregor. Cambridge: Cambridge University Press.

Kittler, F. 1999. *Gramophone, Film, Typewriter*, tr. G. Winthrop-Young & M. Wutz. Stanford: Stanford University Press.

Koyré, A. 1943. "Galileo and the Scientific Revolution of the 17th Century". *The Philosophical Review*, 52(4): 333–348.

Koyré, A. 1957. *From the Closed World to the Infinite Universe*. Baltimore: The John Hopkins Press.

Koyré, A. 1965. *Newtonian Studies*. London: Chapman & Hall.

Kline, M. 1972. *Mathematical Thought From Ancient to Modern Times, vol.3.* New York/Oxford: Oxford University Press.

Kundera, M. 1996. *Testaments Betrayed*, tr. Linda Asher. New York: Harper.

Kundera, M. 2003. *The Art of the Novel*, tr. Linda Asher. New York: Perennial.

Lacan, J. 1999. *Seminar XX, 1972–73, Encore*, tr. B. Fink. New York/London: W.W. Norton & Company.

Lacan, J. 2006. *Écrits: The First Complete Edition in English*, tr. B. Fink. New York/ London: W.W. Norton & Company.

Lacan, J. 2007. *Seminar XVII, The Other Side of Psychoanalysis*, tr. R. Grigg. New York/London: W.W. Norton & Company.

Larese, C. 2015. "Robert Musil: Mathematics as the Audacity of Pure Ratio". *Lettera Matematica*, 2(4): 223–228.

McBride, P. 2006. *The Void of Ethics: Robert Musil and the Experience of Modernity.* Evanston: Northwestern University Press.

McManus, D. 2006. *The Enchantment of Words. Wittgenstein's 'Tractatus Logico-Philosophicus'.* Oxford/New York: Oxford University Press.

Miller, A. I. 2001. *Einstein, Picasso, Space, Time, and the Beauty That Causes Havoc*. New York: Perseus.

Miller, J. 1993. *The Passion of Michel Foucault*. New York: Anchor.

Miller, J.-A. 2003. "Irony: A Contribution of Schizophrenia to the Analytic Clinic". *(Re)-turn: A Journal of Lacanian Studies*, 1: 9–33.

Miller, J.A. 2004. "A Fantasy". http://2012.congresoamp.com/en/template.php?file=Textos/Conferencia-de-Jacques-Alain-Miller-en-Comandatuba.html (Accessed 2 April 2016).

Milner, J.-C. 1996–1997. "Lacan and Modern Science". *Journal of European Psychoanalysis*, 3–4. http://www.psychomedia.it/jep/number3-4/milner.htm (Accessed 10 October 2015).

Milner, J.-C. 2000. "The Doctrine of Science". *Umbr(a), A Journal of the Unconscious: Science and Truth, 2000*: 33–63.

Moffitt, J. F. 2003. *Alchemist of the Avant-Garde, The case of Marcel Duchamp.* New York: SUNY.

Musil, R. 1996. *The Man Without Qualities*, tr. S. Wilkins. New York: Vintage House.

Musil, R. 2001. *The Confusions of Young Törless*, tr. S. Whiteside. London/New York: Penguin.

Nebeker, F. 1995. *Calculating the Weather. Meteorology in the 20th Century*. San Diego: Academic Press.

Nietzsche, F. 2006. *On the Genealogy of Morality*, tr. C. Diethe. Cambridge/New York: Cambridge University Press.

Nietzsche, F. 2007a. *The Anti-Christ, Ecce Homo, Twilight of the Idols, and Other Writings*, tr. J. Norman. Cambridge: Cambridge University Press.

Nietzsche, F. 2007b. *The Gay Science*, tr. J. Nauckhoff. Cambridge: Cambridge University Press.

Parker, A. J. 2007. *Narrative Form and Chaos Theory in Sterne, Proust, Woolf, and Faulkner*. New York: Palgrave Macmillan.

Payne, P. 1988. *Robert Musil's 'Man without Qualities'. A Critical Study*. New York: Cambridge University Press.

Petruccioli, S. 1994. *Atoms, Metaphors, and Paradoxes. Niels Bohr and the Construction of a New Physics*. London/New York: Cambridge University Press.

Plato. 2002. *Phaedrus*, tr. R. Waterfield. Oxford/New York: Oxford University Press.

Plotnitsky, A. 2002. *The Knowable and the Unknowable. Modern Science, Non-Classical Thought, and the Two Cultures*. Ann Arbor: University of Michigan Press.

Rabaté, J. M. 2007. *1913: The Cradle of Modernism*. Oxford: Blackwell Publishing.

Robbin, T. 2006. *The Fourth Dimension in Relativity, Cubism, and Modern Thought*. New Haven/London: Yale University Press.

Schrödinger, E. 2014. *Nature and the Greeks & Science and Humanism*. Cambridge: Cambridge University Press.

Sebastian, T. 2005. The *Intersection of Science and Literature in Musil's 'Man without Quantities'*. New York: Camden House.

Snow, C.P. 1998. *The Two Cultures*. New York: Cambridge University Press.

Spencer, M. 2008. *In the Shadow of Empire: Austrian Experiences of Modernity in the writings of Musil, Roth and Bachmann*. Rochester, NY: Camden House.

Stewart, I. 2002. *Does God Play Dice? The New Mathematics of Chaos*. Oxford: Willey-Blackwell.

Tayler-Turner, Z. 2014. *Philosophy, Literature, and the Dissolution of the Subject. Nietzsche, Musil, Atay*. Frankfurt am Main: Peter Lang Edition.

Thiher, A. 2005. *Fiction Refracts Science. Modernist Writers from Proust to Borges*. Missouri: University of Missouri Press.

Watt, A. 2011. *The Cambridge Introduction to the Work of Marcel Proust*. Cambridge/New York: Cambridge University Press.

Witham, L. 2013. *Picasso and the Chess Player. Pablo Picasso, Marcel Duchamp, and the Battle for the Soul of the Modern Art*. Hanover/London: University Press of New England.

Wittgenstein, L. 2001. *Tractatus Logico-Philosophicus*, tr. D. F. Pears, B. F. McGuinness. London/New York: Routledge.

Zaller, R. 2005. "Robert Musil and the Novel of Metastasis". In H. Bloom (ed.), *Robert Musil's The Man without Qualities*. Philadelphia: Chelsea House.

CHAPTER 10

Genealogy and the Question of the Present: A Conclusion?

Abstract In the final chapter, the emphasis is put on the relation between the critical discourse and the genealogical reading of history under a materialist and historical perspective, in order to raise questions regarding the current syntax of power relations and knowledge in the historical conjuncture of neoliberal *homo œconomicus*.

Keywords Marx • Nietzsche • Lacan • Foucauldian genealogy • *Homo œconomicus* • Materialism

In order to situate the question about the relation between language and reality, namely, the problem of reality and the sign-convention system of representation, in the historical conjuncture of contemporary "information societies", we should recall the Lacanian warning regarding language: "The language apparatus is there somewhere in the brain, like a spider. It has a hold. That might shock you, and you might ask 'Oh come on, really, what are you talking about, where does this language come from?' I have no idea. I'm under no obligation to know everything. And besides, you don't know anything about it either" (2008: 28–33). It might be rather "shocking" that Lacan used "spider" as a metaphor for "language", although our societies are totally wrapped up by the World Wide *Web* of communication, *repressing* (psychoanalytically) the fact that, after Shannon's focus on the mathematics of information and the digitisation of

T. Lagios et al., *Borders, Bodies and Narratives of Crisis in Europe*,
https://doi.org/10.1007/978-3-319-75586-1_10

communication, not only "media is the message", as McLuhan declared, but also controls "all understanding and its illusions", as Kittler claimed (1999: xl; Gane 2005). This metaphor still sounds "shocking", although Nietzsche had *already* and repeatedly used it to describe this daily *repression* of the conditions of possibility of our communication: "The habits of our senses have woven us into lies and deception of sensation: these again are the basis of all our judgments and 'knowledge' – there is absolutely no escape, no backway or bypath into the real world! We sit within our *net*, we *spiders*, and whatever we may catch in it, we can catch nothing at all except that which allows itself to be caught in precisely our net" (1997: II, §117; emphasis added).[1] Or, it might sound rather "shocking" our reference to psychoanalysis regarding the question of language and reality. Nevertheless, this shock has *already* been expressed during the famous Macy Conferences,[2] where many debates concerning the relation between humans and machines took place, but the more passionate and turbulent were those generated by psychoanalysis. Nevertheless, Norbert Wiener, while he was the one who gave scientific status to the signifier "cybernetics", "made it clear that he had no essential objection to psychoanalysis but simply believed that it needed to be rewritten in the language of information, communication, and feedback" (Johnston 2008: 66).

Thus, it should not be "shocking" that this rewriting was realised by Lacan's pen, as he gradually became familiar with the questions and problems of Cybernetics (ibid: 65–67; Liu 2010).[3] It should be more shocking that Lacan rejected steadfastly the *metaphysical* question of *origin*, situating language in a place (of a structure) and confessing that the knowledge of the *origin* can be attained by no*body*. For, only a subject that could know everything and be situated *outside* Hi*story*, would be capable of knowing the *origin* of language itself. Namely, since every attempt to fix

[1] Nietzsche's repeated use of this metaphor stands for "concepts, which capture and organize sensations; or habits that constrain us without being noticed; systems of ideas or practices (both religious and philosophical) and which in the end offer no real support" (Burngham 2015: 307). See, also Constancio and Branco (2012).

[2] A series of postwar conferences (1946–1953), held in New York, sponsored by the Macy Foundation, and aimed at breaking down disciplinary barriers in the sciences, resulting in the launching of the newborn science of Cybernetics (Kline 2015).

[3] It is worth mentioning that Wiener himself visited Paris in 1950 to give a lecture at the Collège de France, as a detailed and penetrating review of Wiener's *Cybernetics: or, Control and Communication in the Animal and the Machine* had appeared in *Le Monde* on 28 December 1948, introducing his thought to France.

the origin of language must be done in language, only a non-human or divine subject could be *outside language* or h*istory*. Consequently, a *materialist* perspective should assert that "there is no metalanguage that can be spoken, or, more aphoristically, there is no Other of the Other" (Lacan 2006: 688). Instead of making navel-gazing exercises in the *inside* of language, it is more useful to analyse the historical intertwinement between language and its own conditions of possibility, namely, between discourse and its own history. As Foucault remarked, Nietzsche, Marx and Freud changed the sign's nature and modified its interpretation by focusing on "a dimension that could be called that of depth, as long as this is not taken to mean interiority, but on the contrary exteriority". It is this *exteriority* that revealed interpretation's incompleteness, since "there is never an *interpretandum* that is not already *interpretans*" (1998a: 272–5). Consequently, these aforementioned "masters of suspicion", instead of inventing a new sign-convention system of representation, subverted the dichotomy between inside *and* outside regarding subject, reality and its representation, and thusly criticised their historical present.[4]

This materialist perspective is irrevocably historical, since Marx demonstrated that there is an immediate continuity between commodity language *and* human language, articulated in the symptom of commodity fetishism; for, there is a structural difference between the psychological or empirical subject of cognition implied by "use-value" and the decentralised or metonymic subject of "exchange value" (Tomŝiç 2015: 27–47).[5] This materialist perspective shows that any analysis focusing exclusively on the *inside* of language, namely, on its propositional logic, discovers only trivialities and tautologies, as Wittgenstein claimed (Monk 1991: 298), and forms paradoxes, because "whatever might be the interpretation or the power of a logical Language, there exists at least one entity which escapes it, which is this Language itself" (Milner 1991: 103). By being simultaneously *historical*, this materialist perspective shows that an analysis

[4] If Marx revealed capitalism as a *historically* determined process of social *homogenisation* of labour at the level of relations of production, Nietzsche revealed modernity as a *historically* determined process of social *homogenisation* of thought at the level of rationality and practices, whereas Freud revealed bourgeois ethics as a *historically* determined process of social *homogenisation* of sexuality at the level of a biopolitical norm.

[5] This structural difference concerning subjectivity cannot be represented, according to Marx, by mathematics, not even by differential calculus, since they deal "only with quantities and thus with quantitative change which cannot be qualitative, contradictory change", as they non-dialectically exclude *temporality*, namely *history* (Carchedi 2011: 289).

focusing on neither inside nor outside language reveals language as a continuous intertwinement of the inside *and* the outside, namely as a *topological* subversion of the univocal division between inside and outside, an *ex-timacy* like the Möbius strip.[6] This materialist perspective is historical, because it does not appeal to an ideal of language as an Aristotelian communicative *organon*, but it articulates the present historical conjuncture, where "according to cybernetics, the essence of someone or something is not the result of the matter he or it is made up of, but the way it is organized and its relationship with the environment" (Hodges 2004: 90). This materialist perspective is historical, since it focuses on the intertwinement of language and history, namely on the social, cultural, economic and political powers that constitute and impose what is considered as Sense and Logic. As Nietzsche demonstrated, the very act of signification is not merely discursive, but a political one: "a manifestation of the power of the rulers: they say 'this *is* so and so', they set their seal on everything and every occurrence with a sound and thereby take possession of it, as it were" (2006: I, §2; Kofman 1993). And, unless the so-called End of History takes place, signification is an endless process. Consequently, the political and theoretical task of interpretation is also infinite, since "[g]enealogy is gray, meticulous, and patiently documentary. It operates on a field of entangled and confused parchments, on documents that have been scratched over and recopied many times" (Foucault 1998b: 369).[7]

Thusly, if we would like to situate the question about the relation between language and reality in the historical conjuncture of contemporary "information societies" and in materialist terms, we should ignore the metaphysical question of the *origin* of the spider's web that keeps us imprisoned and the idealist perspective of its interior articulation, and raise the more modest *theoretical* question of its *history*, of its artificial inter-

[6] As Evans summarises: "Lacan coins the term *extimité* by applying the prefix *ex* (from *exterieur*, 'exterior') to the French word *intimité* ('intimacy'). The resulting neologism [...] neatly expresses the way in which psychoanalysis problematises the opposition between inside and outside, between container and contained. For example, the real is just as much inside as outside, and the unconscious is not a purely interior psychic system but an intersubjective structure. [...] Furthermore, the centre of the subject is outside; the subject is ex-centric. The structure of extimacy is perfectly expressed in the topology of the Torus and of the Möbius strip" (1996: 59).

[7] For a more detailed discussion of the relation between the Foucauldian genealogy and its theoretical (Nietzschean) and political context (activism after May 1968), see Lagios 2016.

twinement between inside *and* outside.[8] If "subjectivity has no relation to the real, but rather to a syntax which is engendered by the signifying mark there" (Lacan 2006: 38), only by raising the critical question *par excellence*, namely, the question of our present, we could possibly realise that the syntax of the predicate "Capital Controls" has *already* been re-interpreted by *historical* and not *grammato*-logical powers as *adjective + noun* instead of *subject + verb*, constituting thusly from the "outside" what we consider as our "inside", our subjectivity. This syntax that engenders in "us" a signifying mark should be questioned, if we would like to raise the question between language and ourselves in the present historical conjuncture of "crisis". This question could be articulated, in Foucault's terms, as the question of the relation between biopolitical power and neoliberalism (Foucault 2009), namely, as the relation between the syntax of individual and social body in a market, since the neoliberal creation of conditions for the existence of the market presuppose interventions in the social domain, a "policy of society" that involves "actions *on* the *conditions* of the market rather than interventions *in* the market itself" (Hoffman 2014: 108).

The syntax of this "policy of society" has a long history that needs a re-interpretation under a materialist and historical perspective that knows no dichotomy between inside and outside, individual and social body, centre and periphery. If discourse is considered as a historical and not only a logical product, then the exteriority of the specific circumstances of the capitalist global expansion could enter the scene by simply *re*-writing the Master's discourse without *changing* a single word: "[Note by Engels to *Capital*'s third German edition] Today, thanks to the competition on the world market which has grown up since then, we have advanced much further. 'If China', says Mr Stapleton, M.P., to his constituents, 'should become a great manufacturing country, I do not see how the manufacturing population of Europe could sustain the contest without descending to the level of their competitors' (*The Times*, 3 September 1873, p. 8). The desired goal of English capital is no longer Continental wages, oh no, it is Chinese wages!" (Marx 1976: 749, fn. 41). This old-fashioned desire of "descending to the level of competitors" has been *already* realised after the advent of neoliberal globalisation and is intensified nowadays after the 2007-8 financial crisis, since the algorithms of profit rates are creating a

[8] "But everything has become: there are *no eternal facts*, just as there are no absolute truths. Consequently what is needed from now on is *historical philosophizing*, and with it the virtue of modesty" (Nietzsche 2007: I, §2).

new paradox, as the inequality has split economically the world between the richest 1% and the rest. And the Master's discourse could represent reality, if it is simply repeated: as multimillionaire Warren Buffett had *already* admitted not in a leftist pamphlet, but in *The New York Times*, "there's class warfare, all right, but it's my class, the rich class, that's making war, and we're winning" (cited in Stein 2006). Or as Eurogroup's chief, Jeroen Dijsselbloem, recently stated: "We had a banking crisis, a fiscal crisis and we spent lot of the tax-payers' money – in the wrong way, in my opinion – to save the banks" (2017). Buffett's or Dijsselbloem's statements on wages and debts describe inequality as a *structural* feature of capitalism, and not as a *sign* of a humanist or moral crisis, confirming Marx's analysis that there "are two interdependent faces of the same process, which injects the asymmetry between capital and labour-power in the inequality between the creditor and the debtor, and *vice versa*" (Tomŝiç 2015: 214).

It might be interpreted that this inequality subverts the very idea of "Europe". However, a genealogical reading of history and its discourse shows that this inequality is not a symptom of a *crisis*, but the very *foundations* of Europe: "We should never forget that Europe as a juridical-political entity, as a system of diplomatic and political security, is the yoke that the most powerful countries (of this Europe) imposed on Germany every time they tried to make it forget the dream of the sleeping emperor, whether Charlemagne, Barbarossa, or the little man who was burnt between his dog and his mistress one May evening on the chancellery premises. Europe is the way of making Germany forget the Empire" (Foucault 2007: 304). This could be a materialist re-interpretation of Europe, which—in a seemingly schizophrenic manner—intensifies and expands the social practices of the capitalist form of debt relation, while, at the same time, the EU motto *In varietate Concordia* attempts to appeal to the humanist ideals. As Deleuze and Guattari eloquently and critically described this relation between *capitalism*, *crisis* and *subject*: "[t]he infinite creditor and infinite credit have replaced the blocks of mobile and finite debts. There is always a monotheism on the horizon of despotism: the debt becomes a *debt of existence*, a debt of the existence of the subjects themselves. A time will come when the creditor has not yet lent while the debtor never quits repaying, for repaying is a duty but lending is an option-as in Lewis Carroll's song, the long song about the infinite debt: *A man may surely claim his dues:/But, when there's money to be lent,/A man must be allowed to choose/Such times as are convenient*" (2000: 197–8). This could be a materialist re-interpretation of the Eurogroups and the so-called negotiations between debtors and creditors. Or, as Nietzsche put it regarding the construction of *memory*: "'How do you give a memory to the animal, man? How do you impress something upon this partly dull, partly idiotic, inattentive mind, this personification of forgetfulness, so that it will stick?' … This age-old question was not resolved with gentle solutions and methods, as can be imagined; perhaps there is nothing more terrible and strange in man's prehistory than his *technique of mnemonics*" (2006: II, §2). This could be a materialist re-interpretation of the infamous *memorandum*[9] and its austerity in a Europe divided between North and South or between humans and *pigs*.[10]

Now, we can see why Engels neither had to change a single word in the dominant discourse, in order to understand his present conjuncture under a materialist perspective, nor did he need to read psychoanalytic texts in order to realise the way language relates to reality: "The huckstering spirit penetrates the whole language, all relations are expressed in business terms, in economic categories. Supply and demand are the formulas according to which the logic of the English bourgeois judges all human life. Hence free competition in every respect, hence the regime of *laissez-faire*, *laissez-aller* in government, in medicine, in education, and before long in religion, too, as the State Church collapses more and more" (2009: 227). Now, in the historical juncture of the "societies of control", where the collapse of the State Church has been almost completed and where "we are taught that businesses have souls" (Deleuze 1992), we can *also* see that "souls are business", since *homo œconomicus* is the new species in the age of post-humanist post-capitalism: "The impersonal voice of a fluctuating 'market' emerges whispering: you should enjoy and live in harmony with your credit. But if you do, be ready for the failing effects of this enjoyment, your condition of indebtedness! Or, conversely: you should abstain from enjoyment in times of austerity, yet, shame on you if you do abstain, as you are not helping your economy!" (Mura 2015). Additionally, we can *also* see that the historical *sine qua non* of the relation between souls and business and between language and reality has been the body's transformation as a field of financial enterprise through the biopolitical

[9] Etymology shows that *memorandum* is every agreement that should be remembered or stick to memory (OED "Memorandum").

[10] PIGS: the unflattering and derogatory—if not racist—acronym of the weak and indebted European economies (Portugal, Italy, Greece, Spain) was invented in the mid-1990s, *long before* the debt crisis of 2008 (Dainotto 2007: 2).

science *par excellence*: medicine. For, in 1937, Dr. Bernard Fantus borrowed the term "bank" from the world of finance to describe the organisation of stored blood in his hospital, which he sought to manage like money in the bank declaring that "the term 'blood bank' is not a mere metaphor" (cited in Swanson 2014: 1). Biopolitics proved to be fertile, as soon as sperm followed blood in the banking system, but capitalism's egalitarian spirit had already been proved by the year of the 1929 crash, when 20 milk banks operated in United States storing and selling breast milk as a "therapeutic merchandise" (Golden 1996).

Thus, the question regarding language and reality should be raised again as an attempt to re-interpret the dominant chain of the signifiers in the present historical conjuncture of crisis and to raise questions about the dominant political syntax and capitalist signification that *punctuate* our subjectivities. If money is "the signifier that most thoroughly annihilates every signification" (Lacan 2006: 27), then it might not be surprising the persistence of the false dilemma between a capitalist or a humanist crisis and the quantification of our subjectivities. What is truly surprising and what should be questioned is that the "naturalness" of human species in the artificial sphere of modernity was a question raised by liberalism not in terms of *ideology*, but in terms of a *technology of power*. This is the reason why Foucault in his work entitled *History of Sexuality* did not focus on the gender identities, but on the *technology* of power and its mechanisms that construct our body and entrap our mind, as "in political thought and analysis, we still have not cut off the head of the king" (Foucault 1978: 88–9). Maybe, the present crisis as a crisis of the present offers the opportunity to raise, once again, the question of the contemporary syntax of *capitalism, crisis and subject*, in terms of a *historical and philosophical* critique of modernity, ignoring any abstract dilemma such as "capitalist or humanist crisis?", and focusing on the *historical exteriority* of Subject and not on its *idealised* essence. Maybe, it offers the opportunity to turn our gaze to our subjectivity by re-interpreting its capitalist signification and opening the possibility for a new one, keeping in mind that "all philosophers have the common failing of starting out from man as he is now and thinking they can reach their goal through an analysis of him. They involuntarily think of 'man' as an *aeterna veritas* [everlastingly true], as something that remains constant in the midst of all flux, as a sure measure of things. Everything the philosopher has declared about man is, however, at bottom no more than a testimony as to the man of a very limited period of time. Lack of historical sense is the family failing of all philosophers" (Nietzsche 2007: I, §2).

References

Burngham, D. 2015. *The Nietzsche Dictionary*. London/New Delhi/New York/ Sydney: Bloomsbury.

Carchedi, G. 2011. *Behind the Crisis. Marx's Dialectics of Value and Knowledge*. London/Boston: Brill.

Costanzio, J. and Branco Mayer, M.J. 2012. *As the Spider Spins. Essays on Nietzsche's Critique and Use of Language*. Boston/Berlin: De Gruyter.

Dainotto, R.M. 2007. *Europe (in Theory)*. Durham/London: Duke University Press.

Deleuze, G. 1992. "Postscript on the Societies of Control". *October*, 59: 3–7.

Deleuze, G. and Guattari, F. 2000. *Anti-Oedipus, Capitalism and Schizophrenia*, tr. by R. Hurley, M. Seem and H. R. Lane. Minneapolis: University of Minnesota Press.

Dijsselbloem, J. 2017. European Parliament's Employment and Social Affairs Committee. http://www.europarl.europa.eu/ep-live/en/committees/video?event=20171109-0900-COMMITTEE-EMPL#managehelp (Accessed 9 November 2017).

Engels, F. 2009. *The Condition of the Working-Class in England in 1844*, V. Kiernan (ed.). London: Penguin.

Evans, D. 1996. *An Introductory Dictionary of Lacanian Psychoanalysis*. London: Routledge.

Foucault, M. 1978. *The History of Sexuality, vol. I*, tr. R. Hurley. New York: Pantheon.

Foucault, M. 1998a. "Nietzsche, Freud, Marx". In *Essential Works of Foucault, 1954–1984, vol. 2: Aesthetics*, tr. Robert Hurley & others. London: Penguin.

Foucault, M. 1998b. "Nietzsche, Genealogy, History". In *Essential Works of Foucault, 1954–1984, vol. 2: Aesthetics*, tr. Robert Hurley & Others. London: Penguin.

Foucault, M. 2007. *Security, Territory, Population, Lectures at the Collège de France, 1977–78*, tr. by G. Burchell. New York: Palgrave Macmillan.

Foucault, M. 2009. *The Birth of Biopolitics, Lectures at the Collège de France, 1978–79*, tr. by G. Burchell. New York: Palgrave Macmillan.

Gane, N. 2005. "Radical Post-humanism. Friedrich Kittler and the Primacy of Technology". *Theory, Culture & Society*, 22(3): 25–41. https://doi.org/10.1177/0263276405053718.

Golden, J. 1996. *A Social History of Wet Nursing in America. From Breast to Bottle*. Cambridge: Cambridge University Press.

Johnston, J. 2008. *The Allure of Machinic Life. Cybernetics, Artificial Life, and the New AI*. Massachusetts/London: MIT Press.

Hodges, A. 2004. *Alan Turing: Life and Legacy of a Great Thinker*. New York: Springer.

Hoffman, M. 2014. *Foucault and Power. The Influences of Political Engagement on Theories of Power*. New York/London/New Delhi/Sydney: Bloomsbury.

Kittler, F. 1999. *Gramophone, Film, Typewriter*, tr. G. Winthrop-Young & M. Wutz. Stanford: Stanford University Press.

Kline, R. 2015. *Cybernetics Moment*. Baltimore: Johns Hopkins University Press.

Kofman, S. 1993. *Nietzsche and Metaphor*, tr. D. Large. London: Athlone Press.

Lacan, J. 2006. *Écrits. The First Complete Edition*, tr. B. Fink. New York/London: W.W. Norton & Company.

Lacan, J. 2008. *My Teaching*, tr. D. Macey. London/New York: Verso.

Lagios, T. 2016. "Foucauldian Genealogy and Maoism". *Le foucaldien, 2/1*, https://doi.org/10.16995/lefou.12.

Liu, H. L. 2010. "The Cybernetic Unconscious: Rethinking Lacan, Poe, and French Theory". *Critical Inquiry*, 36(2): 288–320.

Marx, K. 1976. *Capital, vol. 1*, tr. B. Fowkes. London: Penguin.

Milner, J.-C. 1990. *For the Love of Language*, tr. A. Banfield. New York: Palgrave Macmillan.

Monk, R. 1991. Ludwig Wittgenstein. *The Duty of Genius*. London/New York: Penguin.

Mura, A. 2015. "Lacan and Debt: The Discourse of the Capitalist in times of Austerity". *Philosophy Today*, 59(2): 155–174. https://doi.org/10.5840/philtoday201521958.

Nietzsche, F. 1997. *Daybreak*, tr. R.J. Hollingdale. Cambridge/New York: Cambridge University Press.

Nietzsche, F. 2006. *On the Genealogy of Morality*, tr. C. Diethe. Cambridge/New York: Cambridge University Press.

Nietzsche, F. 2007. *Human, All Too Human*, tr. R. J. Holingdale. Edinbrugh/New York: Cambridge University Press.

Online Etymology Dictionary. "Memorandum". https://www.etymonline.com/word/memorandum (Accessed 24 September 2015).

Stein, B. 2006. "In Class Warfare, Guess Which Class Is Winning". http://www.nytimes.com/2006/11/26/business/yourmoney/26every.html (Accessed 20 November 2014).

Swanson, K. W. 2014. *Banking on the Body. The Market in Blood, Milk and Sperm in Modern America*. Cambridge, MA/London: Harvard University Press.

Tomšiç, S. 2015. *The Capitalist Unconscious: Marx and Lacan*. London/New York: Verso.

Afterword

Our book was an attempt to raise questions regarding a series of interrelated issues revolving around the concept of the "crisis" and the dominant narratives on it. Namely, it is about a concept that, due to the dominant discourse and the established practices that daily build an exceptionally successful consensus mechanism, is rarely subjected to any historicalisation or critique regarding its political, social and epistemological conditions of possibility. Consequently, the unrestrained multiplication and the constant reproduction of various significations of the "crisis" dominate every aspect of everyday life: financial crisis, debt crisis, migration crisis, humanist crisis, political crisis, identity crisis ... Paradoxically, it is usually forgotten that, under the signifier "crisis", a harsh reality—beyond the realm of discourse—is taking shape: war conflicts and "waves" of bodies that seek refuge in the Western world after struggling successfully with the sea waves in the Aegean Sea, other bodies being washed up dead, thousands of migrants living in deplorable conditions in concentration camps, austerity measures and memoranda, wage cuts, houses' forfeiture, impoverishment of a large part of society, are events that are considered, among many others, as preposterous under the humanist perspective and beyond the discourse of "humanitarian aid" or humanist morality, on the one hand, and that have been rendered the *norm* in the state of exception due to the so-called crisis, on the other hand. For, this norm has been established on a neoliberal financial rationality that renders *homo œconomicus* the only species that has a "body that matters".

T. Lagios et al., *Borders, Bodies and Narratives of Crisis in Europe*,
https://doi.org/10.1007/978-3-319-75586-1

The questions raised in this book attempted to shed light on specific aspects, obscured in the shadow produced by the bright light of the screens that are filled with spectacular media coverage and over-information about the crisis, but are lacking of critique. In other words, how is borders' transformation and diffusion related to the creation of an obedient, multinational working class *inside* the West? In which ways does the construction of "humanist crises" and "states of emergency" render certain migration policies as the only "viable solutions", excluding, at the same time, any critique or discussion for alternatives? In which ways are borders literally incorporated into the human body itself, at the beginning of the twenty-first century? How have the capitalist and the humanist crisis been intertwined as the two sides of the same coin or as the continuous surface of a Möbius strip avoiding any critical discussion of their genealogy?

Despite the fact that these questions are inevitably imbued with the authors' political stances and epistemological views, the goal of this book was, in no way, to present or propose a series of absolute and ready-made solutions, but to *deconstruct* an ostensibly seamless description of reality, with the hope that these questions could mark a path towards the agony of the very victims of the "crisis" and the questions that agonise the very subjects of history, and not a linkage with all those who keep propagating the "End of History"; that is, all those who, as T. Pynchon puts it, in *Gravity's Rainbow*,"[i]f they can get you asking the wrong questions, they don't have to worry about answers". Thus, our questions are inevitably left without definite answers, since these could only be articulated by all those who cannot find their experience of crisis signified by the established chain of signifiers that, in the present historical conjuncture, under the pretext or guise of humanist ideals, conceals and leads to the oblivion the chain of signifiers that marks everyday life in the West: *capitalism, crisis, subject*. For, capitalism and its crises keep haunting their subjects like a *spectre*, as Adorno remarked in his *Minima Moralia*: "For while bourgeois forms of existence are truculently conserved, *their economic pre-condition has fallen away*. Privacy has given way entirely to the privation it always secretly was, and with the stubborn adherence to particular interests is now mingled fury at being no longer able to perceive that things might be different and better. In losing their innocence, the bourgeois have become impenitently malign. The caring hand that even now tends the little garden as if it had not long since become a 'lot', *but fearfully wards off the unknown intruder, is already that which denies the political refugee asylum*. Now objectively threatened, the subjectivity of the rulers and their hangers-on *becomes totally inhuman*. So the class realizes itself, taking upon itself the destructive will of the course of the world. The bourgeois live on like *spectres* threatening doom" (emphasis added).

All in all, without having the illusion that after Auschwitz a new, universal moral system or a *Magna Moralia* could be articulated, we made an attempt to *question* the humanist ethics that believes in the progress of morality, while, at the same time, represses to oblivion the subjects that have *already* been condemned to death in front of the borders and control mechanisms, or excluded due to the debt crisis of late capitalism, incorporating the *spectre* that is still threatening and ordering *life*...

The rest is silence ...

Index[1]

[1] Note: Page number followed by 'n' refers to notes.

T. Lagios et al., *Borders, Bodies and Narratives of Crisis in Europe*,
https://doi.org/10.1007/978-3-319-75586-1

The manufacturer's authorised representative in the EU is Springer Nature Customer Service Centre GmbH, Europaplatz 3, 69115 Heidelberg, Germany. If you have any concerns regarding our products, please contact ProductSafety@springernature.com

Printed and bound by CPI Group (UK) Ltd, Croydon, CR0 4YY

25/09/2026

02222890-0016